PRAISE FOR

JESUS UNDEFEATED

"There is a growing body of work in Christian literature supporting the doctrine of universal reconciliation. Keith Giles' *Jesus
Undefeated* is indeed the perfect introduction to the idea that all
shall be saved. Simply written without suffering from too much
brevity, the author not only puts forth a convincing case that
Universalism should be accepted at the theological table, but
that it is perhaps the most likely answer to the question, 'Who
then shall be saved?'"

— MATTHEW J. DISTEFANO, AUTHOR OF 5 BOOKS AND CO-HOST OF
THE *HERETIC HAPPY HOUR PODCAST*

"Citing scripture, ancient Church leaders, and contemporary
biblical scholars, Keith Giles makes a compelling case against
hell. What makes this book especially winsome is the accessible
way Giles writes. The conversation is easy to follow and argu-
ments compelling. This book is both an encyclopedic resource
and conversation starter!"

— THOMAS JAY OORD, AUTHOR OF *GOD CAN'T: HOW TO BELIEVE
IN GOD AND LOVE AFTER TRAGEDY, ABUSE, AND OTHER EVILS*
AND *THE UNCONTROLLING LOVE OF GOD*

"Sometimes you *can* judge a book by its cover, or at least its title. Keith Giles' newest book title says it all—*Jesus Undefeated: Condemning the False Doctrine of Eternal Torment.*

The title is a messianic manifesto which boldly declares that God's indefatigable "will-to-all-goodness" *shall*, without creaturely exception or divine reservation, woo and win *all* humanity to salvation. For many, this victory may come in this current earth age, or it may manifest in the postmortem ages to come. But, Keith assures us, come it most assuredly shall. "Simply put, Jesus' will to rescue, reconcile and restore *all* of us will not and cannot be eternally thwarted. Delayed sure, but never ultimately prevented. God is both an irresistible force and an immovable object on this vital matter. He always finds, rescues, and defends His lost sheep. After connecting the dynamic dots in his first three books of a flawlessly good natured God of light and love, Keith now confronts the remaining conceptual Goliath "blocking the pass" of Christian unity and growth. This inner Goliath, which stalks every human heart, is an irrational fear coupled with a toxic conviction that God eternally tortures and consciously torments those who never believe or receive Him during their earthly lives. Keith picks up the same Davidic slingshot used by the Patristic leaders of the early church to decapitate this Goliath once and for all. *Jesus Undefeated* takes us on a briskly paced survey of the early church fathers, the ancient Scriptures, and Keith's own folksy wisdom on this challenging topic.

Keith's writings are so accessible. It's one of his greatest gifts, along with his tight reasoning and honey-smooth prose. Just as in the famous fable of *The Three Little Pigs* where the straw and wooden houses couldn't withstand strong winds, so too do the two alternate views of Hell likewise collapse under Keith's sage scrutiny. These two alternate views of Hell are known as 1) eternal conscious torment (the lost are eternally tortured), and 2) annihilationism (the lost are incinerated into nothing-ness). Keith leaves these two theories in scattered piles of decon-structed debris as he presents the indestructible brick house of universalism which the early church built in the immediate cen-turies following Christ's incarnation. And that house can't be blown down, no matter how rough are the winds of wrath which seek to assail it.

Jesus Undefeated reveals an early church corpus who, through their common sense and sacred intuition, knew what we moderns seem to have so inexplicably forgotten. They corpo-rately knew God far too well to believe Him capable of *ever* creating such a bone-torturing Hell. After reading Keith's *Jesus Undefeated,* we too will know better than to believe in the anti-Gospel which promotes the "double barrel shotgun" threat of an endlessly Hellish torture chamber where the bulk of human-ity suffers eternal conscious torment at the hands of God who claims to be only love and light.

This lie needs to fry. And Keith, as a master conceptual chef, does just that in his wonderful new book which I heartily recommend."

— RICHARD MURRAY, AUTHOR OF *GOD VERSUS EVIL: SCULPTING AN EPIC THEOLOGY OF GOD'S HEROIC GOODNESS* AND *THE QUESTION OF HELL*

OTHER BOOKS BY THE AUTHOR

- *Jesus Unveiled: Forsaking Church as We Know It for Ekklesia as God Intended*

- *Jesus Unbound: Liberating the Word of God from the Bible*

- *Jesus Untangled: Crucifying Our Politics to Pledge Allegiance to the Lamb*

- *The Power of Weakness: How God Loves to Do Extraordinary Things Through Ordinary People*

- *The Gospel: For Here or to Go?*

- *The Top 10 Things Every Christian Should Know (But Probably Doesn't)*

- *Nobody Follows Jesus (So Why Should You?)*

- *[Subversive Interviews] Volume 1*

- *War Is Not Christian*

- *How To Start A Ministry To The Poor In Your Own Community*

Available online at: www.KeithGiles.com

Copyright © 2019 by Keith Giles.

First Edition

Cover design and layout by Rafael Polendo (polendo.net)

Unless otherwise identified, all Scripture quotations in this publication are taken from the Holy Bible, New International Version®, NIV®. Copyright ©1973, 1978, 1984, 2011 by Biblica, Inc.™ Used by permission of Zondervan. All rights reserved worldwide. www.zondervan.com The "NIV" and "New International Version" are trademarks registered in the United States Patent and Trademark Office by Biblica, Inc.™

ESV Bible® (The Holy Bible, *English Standard Version*®), copyright © 2001 by Crossway Bibles, a publishing ministry of Good News Publishers. Used by permission. All rights reserved. www.crossway.org.

ISBN 978-1-938480-47-8

This volume is printed on acid free paper and meets ANSI Z39.48 standards.

Printed in the United States of America

QUOIR

Published by Quoir
Orange, California

www.quoir.com

JESUS
UNDEFEATED
CONDEMNING THE FALSE DOCTRINE OF ETERNAL TORMENT

KEITH GILES

SPECIAL THANKS

Rafael Polendo, Steve Gregg, Richard Murray, Steve Kline, Michael Paul, Matthew Distefano, Mark Vanskiver, and Wendy Giles.

DEDICATION

To Gene and Joyce Giles, my parents, who have always supported me and encouraged me to keep writing.

TABLE OF CONTENTS

FOREWORD

*"O Death, where is your sting? O Hell, where is your victory? Christ
is risen, and you are overthrown. Christ is risen, and the demons are
fallen. Christ is risen, and the angels rejoice. Christ is risen, and life
reigns. Christ is risen, and not one dead remains in the grave. For
Christ, being risen from the dead, is become the first fruits of those
who have fallen asleep. To Him be glory and dominion unto ages of
ages. Amen."*

—ST. JOHN CHRYSOSTOM'S PASCHAL HOMILY

Certain of the church fathers, including St. John of Antioch
(quoted above), were fond of employing hellfire rhetoric in their
homilies, especially when directed at the corrupt Empress and
her powerful entourage. John seemed to think the fear-monger-
ing approach was effective, but multiple banishments make that
claim seem dubious. Maybe it was just cathartic. Even if threats
of an eternal furnace seem to work, is a gospel of fear and punishment congruent with the "perfect Love that drives out fear of
punishment"? Of course it isn't.

For John of Antioch, when it came down to the most crucial
message of the year, the message of Christ's resurrection delivered at the midnight Passover feast, we hear an entirely different
voice. His proclamation of Christ's universal victory over death

and *hades* was unequivocal: *"Christ is risen, and not one dead remains in the grave!"* For these bold words of extravagant good news—now preached in all Eastern Orthodox Churches across the world every year until the Lord returns—John would earn the name, "Golden Mouth."

In *Jesus Undefeated*, Giles makes a case for the reality of a Universalist stream flowing through the first centuries of the early church. It was not the *only* point of view, but neither was it rare nor considered heretical.

For example, St. Gregory of Nyssa, the "father of the fathers" and "flower of Orthodoxy", was not only an ardent Universalist— he also ensured that at the Second Ecumenical Council, the final form of the "Symbol of Faith" (our Creed), proclaimed "the life of the age to come." Period.

Eternal conscious torment is simply not part of the Christian dogma—just as it had never once been mentioned in the evangelism of the Book of Acts. Not once.

So, while the Infernalist position would later dominate Christianity for sixteen centuries, it is a cringe-worthy misnomer to call it the "traditional view." Like so many of our ugliest old Christian "traditions," eternal conscious torment picked up steam by way of the medieval imagination and then via Protestant literalism. That half-baked recipe came out of the oven as Evangelical Revivalist preaching and Jonathan Edward's "Sinners in the Hands of an Angry God."

We still haven't recovered.

How is it that otherwise mentally stable Christ-followers can cling to such an egregious vision of the afterlife when we've received such a glorious gospel? It's only possible in the context of their notion of faithfulness. If you've been told that letting go of the Lake of Fire means taking sin lightly, turning from Christ, walking away from the Cross, and forgetting the final judgement and afterlife—well, those are too many convictions to give up. And worse, it's far too great a gamble for most. Because, what if you're wrong and end up on the wrong end of the last verdict?

The challenge becomes whether you should risk hell by not believing in hell and by failing to preach about hell. If we don't, what happens to those who are no longer afraid of damnation? What? Shall we preach grace that sin might abound? (See, Paul was up against the same objection.)

Well, that type of wager argument might have worked for 18th century circuit riders, but the question is reversed today. Instead, we need to ask, "Shall we continue preaching hell if preaching hell is causing people to reject Christ?" Because, ironically, Infernalism creates *far* more atheists than it converts!

Sadly, when fear of hell is off the table, many do seem to lose their faith in Christ altogether. But, then, was their faith in Christ in the first place? Or was he just a fire insurance policy peddled by retributive religion—a way out of the bad place, just in case. Such does not constitute faith. But if that's all you've been offered, I guess that's on the preacher's head. Damn.

In this book, Keith Giles will show us how the very foundations of our faith never required eternal conscious torment in the first place. And far from damaging our faith, this original good news brings Christ into central focus so that the love of God revealed in Christ is the point.

What we preach is the Cruciform love of the God who never turns away, and it's also what we experience. Christ's unique revelation is that God *is* love—the One who forgives and redeems and restores us from all the ways we're already enslaved and perishing.

Keith takes Scripture very seriously, and especially the claims of our Lord Jesus Christ and the power of his death and resurrection to conquer death and *hades*. Who knows—I think maybe Keith's even got a bit of that *Golden Mouth* in him too.

Let it flow, brother!

– Brad Jersak

Author of *Her Gates Will Never Be Shut* and *A More Christlike Way: A More Beautiful Faith*.

INTRODUCTION

"There are very many in our day who, though not denying the Holy Scriptures, do not believe in endless torments."

—AUGUSTINE (354 TO 430 A.D.)

How much longer must I bear with these people? He wondered. Lifting his eyes one last time, he scanned the crowd. Were they ready for what was about to come? Would they heed his warnings or face the unquenchable fires of judgement for refusing to repent of their sins?

He was weary. All around him the people stood in a ragged circle. Some laughed under their breath. Some of them clutched their children in fear. Others were just waiting to see if he might work a miracle before his speech was over.

He lowered his head and gathered strength for what would come next. He knew that many of them would gladly turn and kill him if they had the chance. Yet, this is why he was sent: to warn Jerusalem of the coming judgement.

Suddenly the Spirit of God surged within him. He felt his heart begin to swell. His blood rushed like thunder in his ears. His mouth opened. His tongue moved as if it had a mind all its own and out flowed the words of God:

"Let those who have ears to hear listen closely! They who refuse to listen will be thrown into the fires of Gehenna. God will give your bodies as food to the wild birds and beasts of the field. There are those standing here who will not taste death before these words come to pass," he shouted.

"If you will not repent, you will be thrown into the place where the fire is not quenched and where the worm does not die!"

There was an audible gasp from the crowd. They knew what this meant. They were standing in Gehenna already.

Could what this Prophet said be true? Would they all die like this? Would their dead bodies really be stacked up in this valley and burned like trash outside the city gates?

THERE WAS AN AUDIBLE GASP FROM THE CROWD. THEY KNEW WHAT THIS MEANT. THEY WERE STANDING IN GEHENNA ALREADY.

Unfortunately, yes. This is exactly what happened in fulfillment of Jeremiah's prophecy. Just as he had warned them, their city was invaded, their temple destroyed and so many of them were slaughtered that there was nowhere to bury the bodies. So they were thrown into this valley of Gehenna, just outside the city gates, in the same place where they had once offered their children to the idols of Molech.

Jeremiah's prophecy had nothing to do with what would happen to the souls of these inhabitants of Jerusalem after they died in this horrific way. But it had everything to do with how they would die in just a few short days, and what would happen to their dead bodies.

Unfortunately, when Jesus borrowed this very same language to warn the Jewish people in his day about the coming destruction of Jerusalem and the Temple, there were those who failed to connect the dots to the prophecies of Jeremiah and other Old Testament prophets.

Instead, they took the warnings Jesus gave to those people about a specific invasion of their land as being about some future event yet to come at the end of the world. Gehenna became mistranslated as "Hell" rather than as the very real geographical Valley of Hinnom outside of Jerusalem.

The warnings given to those people—whom Jesus said would live to see this destruction in their own lifetime—were applied to everyone in the history of the entire world who didn't become a Christian.

In this way, Gehenna became a place of eternal conscious torment where sinners would burn for all eternity. But why? And how and when did this happen?

The story is one that most Christians have never heard. Many assume that the Church has always believed in an eternal place of conscious torment for those who rebel against God. They are totally unaware that, for the first 500 years of Church history, almost everyone who followed Christ embraced a doctrine of Universalism, or Ultimate Reconciliation.

This book aims to correct this misunderstanding and reintroduce the beautiful Gospel of Patristic Universalism that has always been hidden in plain sight—right there for all to see in the words of Jesus and the Apostle Paul, and in the writings of the early Church Fathers who came after them.

This is a story that few have ever heard, but it is embedded in our DNA. It is woven into the history of the Christian church from the inception.

Are you ready to hear it? We'll begin our journey deep underground, back in time, in the Catacombs of Rome.

Let's go.

CHAPTER 1

A LIGHT IN THE DARKNESS

"The mass of men (Christians) say there is to be an end to punishment and to those who are punished."

—ST. BASIL THE GREAT (329 TO 379 A.D.)

Felix tightened his grip on the torch. He knew his way by heart, but his mind was elsewhere.

Suddenly he stopped. The sound of footsteps behind him slowly faded into silence. "We're almost there," he said. "It's just up ahead, my friends."

He waited as his words had finished echoing softly along the chamber walls. A few people whispered prayers of thanksgiving. Jana, his oldest daughter, placed her hand gently upon his shoulder. In the torchlight, he could see that her eyes were wet with tears, but the smile she gave him warmed his heart. She looked so much like her mother in that moment. He smiled back at her briefly and continued on his way. The people followed.

"It gets tighter in this section," he warned. "Be careful, friends."

Silently they wandered deeper into the Catacombs. Feet shuffling. Heads bowed.

Then, Felix stopped. They were here.

As they looked around, they saw that they were standing in a wider opening. There was a gallery cut into one side of the chamber. Five narrow shelves were arranged one upon the other. Each row was three to five feet apart from the next one. Most were already filled with silent tenants who had made this journey weeks or months before. Many of them they knew by name.

Felix raised his torch to one of the empty shelves cut deep into the side of the rock. "This one," he said.

Silently, the group parted to allow four of them to pass. They carried a large bundle wrapped in a dark cloth between them. Gently, they shuffled forward and lowered the body at the feet of Felix and Jana.

Before anyone else could speak, Jana's voice broke the silence. "We thank you, oh Abba, for my Mother's life. We praise you, Good Shepherd, for your great and bountiful love. Today we rejoice as we give back to you my dear mother, Victoria."

As she spoke, several of them prayerfully added encouragements to her, saying "Amen!" and "Maranatha!"

Jana continued. "Dearest Mother, may you always remain in peace with God, our Beloved Father. Today you are born into Eternity. Today we lay you to rest knowing your soul is alive with Christ in a dream of peace."

Even without the torches they carried, Jana's wide smile was visible in the darkness. Felix, felt such great love for her as he reached out and took her hand in his own.

Then their friends began to speak. One-by-one they each shared their stories of how Victoria's life had reflected the love of God to them. They laughed together and recited scriptures from memory about the life of Christ and the love of God which was higher and wider and longer and deeper than anyone could ever imagine.

When they were done, Felix lifted his head and began to sing loudly. His familiar baritone shook their hearts as his joyful song of praise reverberated throughout the chamber. Immediately each person opened their mouths to join him in a song of rejoicing to celebrate God's goodness and faithfulness. They were not silent now. Their voices were joined as one to boldly proclaim the goodness of God and the promise of life that was theirs in Christ.

As they sang, the walls seemed to vibrate. It was as if the very gates of hell were trembling. Christ was alive, and so, too, was their dear friend, and wife and mother; alive and forever embraced in the arms of God.

In the darkness of this place, surrounded by the unshakable reality of death, these Christians sang songs of great joy and not of gloom; of vibrant life and not of defeat.

When they had finished singing, their voices continued to echo throughout the miles of darkness in every direction.

"We lay your body here, my love," whispered Felix, as they lifted his wife up and into the opening cut in the wall. "Rest well. We will see you again very soon."

Then they all turned and made their way back the way they had come, singing a new song as they went.

When they finally emerged from the Catacombs, the sun was just beginning to rise. They scattered, then, each to their own home, to begin this day with joyful anticipation; eager to see what beautiful thing the Lord might work through them as they remained faithful to His voice.

For over 400 years, scenes like this played out in the underground network of tombs hidden deep

IN THE DARKNESS OF THIS PLACE, SURROUNDED BY THE UNSHAKEABLE REALITY OF DEATH, THESE CHRISTIANS SANG SONGS OF GREAT JOY AND NOT OF GLOOM; OF VIBRANT LIFE AND NOT OF DEFEAT.

beneath the city of Rome. Over 500 miles worth of light shines in this darkness where bodies were laid to rest in hopeful expectancy of the life to come.

At the epitaph of every Christian soul laid to rest here, the inscriptions are fiercely hopeful and defiantly joyful. Every picture carved here is one of beauty and peace. Every sermon in the stone found among the dead is filled with life, not gloom.

In all the drawings and scriptures uncovered along these endless rows of departed saints, not one reference is found of Christ's sufferings or death. Not one cross is carved there. Not one image of His brief moment of torture at the hands of the Romans. Instead, every reference is to Christ as our Good Shepherd, or to His victory over death. Their emphasis in death was optimistically life-affirming and hopeful. Even in their darkest hours, and in their darkest tombs, the life and light of Christ could not be eclipsed.

Keep in mind, these followers of Christ often lived lives of fear above ground. Their daily reality was one of severe persecution by the Roman Empire. Their neighbors lived lives of hedonistic abandon. As one historian put it:

> "The church was born into a world of whose moral rottenness few have or can have any idea. Even the sober historians of the later Roman Empire have their pages tainted with scenes impossible to translate; Lusts the foulest, debauchery to us happily inconceivable, raged on every side. To assert even faintly the final redemption of all this rottenness, whose depths we dare not try to sound, required the firmest faith in the larger hope, as an essential part of the Gospel."[1]

How great this point is, and we would do well not to miss it. Those earliest Christians were hounded, tortured, mocked and murdered in ways we can barely comprehend. So, for them to maintain a sense of joy in the face of such horror was—and is—itself a miracle. Yet, there is an even greater miracle than this: the idea that these same persecuted Christians should embrace Ultimate Reconciliation for everyone—even those who had most cruelly and hatefully tortured and killed their own mothers, fathers, sisters, brothers and children.

The quote continues:

> "But this is not all; in a peculiar sense the Church was militant in the early centuries. It was engaged in, at times, a struggle for life or death, with a relentless persecution. Thus, it must have seemed in that age almost an act of treason to the cross to teach that, though dying unrepentant, the bitter persecutor, or the votary of abominable lusts, should yet in the ages to come find salvation. Such considerations help us to see the extreme weight attaching even to the very least expression in the [Church] Fathers which involves sympathy with the larger hope…"[2]

Yet, in spite of this reality, the early Christians *did* embrace the Gospel of Ultimate Reconciliation, as we will soon see. Their unshakable optimism in the face of death is extended even to the hope of eternal life for those who helped to end their lives prematurely.

This is the astounding, breathtaking beauty of the earliest Christians. We cannot dismiss such boundless hope. We dare not brush aside this brand of extravagant love.

We need it; maybe now more than ever. In a world where hope and love are in such short supply—even among those who name the Name of Christ—such love and hope are more precious and priceless than ever before.

So, let's take some time to explore what the earliest Christians believed about the afterlife, and why.

Most Christians don't realize that there were always three different views held by the Church from the very beginning. What were they? Where did they come from?

That's what we'll discover in our next chapter.

CHAPTER 2

ALWAYS THREE VIEWS

"And God showed great kindness to man, in this, that He did not suffer him to continue being in sin forever; but as it were, by a kind of banishment, cast him out of paradise in order that, having punishment expiated within an appointed time, and having been disciplined, he should afterwards be recalled...just as a vessel, when one being fashioned it has some flaw, is remolded or remade that it may become new and entire; so also it happens to man by death. For he is broken up by force, that in the resurrection he may be found whole...spotless, righteous and immortal."

—THEOPHILUS OF ANTIOCH (183 A.D.)

Most Christians today are oblivious as to how much the Church has shifted on the doctrine of Hell over the centuries.

For example, most assume that there is only one truly "Christian" view of Hell and that would be the doctrine of eternal conscious torment. Anyone who denies this view, or who teaches a different view of Hell, is not only a heretic, he is also "un-Biblical."

One of the main reasons that so many Christians believe this is because their pastors have taught them to react this way. Fear is the number one way to protect your view and to prevent any-one in your church or denomination from listening to any other views than the ones you want them to listen to.

Here's the reality: the Christian church has *always* held three different views of Hell. All three views were "Christian" views, and all three views were based completely on the Bible.

> **HERE'S THE REALITY: THE CHRISTIAN CHURCH HAS ALWAYS HELD THREE DIFFERENT VIEWS OF HELL. ALL THREE VIEWS WERE "CHRISTIAN" VIEWS, AND ALL THREE VIEWS WERE BASED COMPLETELY ON THE BIBLE.**

Those three views were known as: Universal Reconciliation, Eternal Suffering, and Annihilation (or Conditional Immortality).

Note this reference in the New Schaff-Herzog Christian Encyclopedia which says:

"The earliest system of Universalistic theology was by Clement of Alexandria who was the head of the theological school in that city until 202 A.D. His successor in the school was the great Origen, the most distinguished advocate of this doctrine in all time."[1]

"In the first five or six centuries of Christianity there were six known theological schools, of which four (Alexandria, Antioch, Caesarea, and Edessa, or Nisibis) were Universalist; one (Ephesus) accepted conditional immortality; one (Carthage or Rome) taught endless punishment of the wicked."[2]

So, let's summarize what this tells us about the earliest views of Hell:

- There were six theological schools

- Each school was located in a specific city

- Four of those were Universalist schools

- One of the schools taught Conditional Immortality

- One of the schools taught Eternal Suffering

- The school that taught Eternal Suffering was in Rome

These facts are quite eye-opening. First, because we learn that in the first 500 years of Christianity, the majority of Christians believed in universalism. That's quite a shock.

Next, we learn that the other two views—annihilation and eternal suffering—only had one school teaching their doctrine, placing both in a very minority position.

Finally, we see that the one school that taught eternal suffering was located in the city of Rome. Does that tell us anything? Did the city of Rome rise to any sort of prominence in the Christian church around that time? Would that detail help to explain why the other schools were eventually drowned out of the conversation later?

We'll talk about this in more detail soon. For now, let's look at what the earliest Christians had to say about their faith. Because, as the early Christians began to write down their Creeds and statements of belief, it's surprising that none of them felt the need to mention anything about having the correct view of hell as a prerequisite for faith.

In other words: Early Christians disagreed about what happens to people who die without Christ, and they did not consider it heresy to have a view that was different than any other Christian might hold.

As J.W. Hanson notes:

"Thus the Credal declarations of the Christian church for almost four hundred years are entirely void of the lurid doctrine [eternal suffering] with which they afterwards blazed for more than a thousand years. The early Creeds contain no hint of it [eternal suffering], and no whisper of condemnation of the doctrine of Universal Restoration as taught by Clement, Origen, the Gregories, Basil, the Great, and multitudes besides....The reticence of all the ancient formularies of faith concerning end-less punishment at the same time that the Great Fathers were proclaiming Universal Salvation...is strong evidence that the former doctrine was not then accepted. It is apparent that the early Christian church did not dogmatize on man's final destiny....It is insupposable that endless punishment was a doctrine of the early church, when it is seen that not one of the early creeds embodied it."[3]

Two things must be noted here before we continue:

First, the fact that endless punishment was not mentioned in the Creeds does not prove that none of the early Christians held that view. As we have already noted, some of them did embrace that view.

Second, while the earliest creeds did not contain references to eternal suffering, they also contain no condemnation of universal reconciliation. And for good reason, because *most of those who helped to write those earliest creeds embraced the doctrine of universalism.*

In fact, Gregory of Nazianzen, who presided over the Council in Constantinople where the Nicene Creed was finally crafted, was himself a universalist. And Gregory of Nyssa added this phrase to the creed: *"I believe in the life of the world to come,"* which affirmed his own convictions regarding universal reconciliation.

So, as we consider these facts, let me ask you: can you imagine a gathering of Christian leaders today who would allow an openly universalist Christian to preside over the meeting? Can you imagine that council allowing other universalists to sit on that same council and to shape a creed that they would all agree to? How would this even be possible unless those early Christians (in 381 A.D.) had no strong feelings about the doctrine of Hell, and had no problems with universalist doctrines being freely expressed?

As J.W. Hanson again remarks:

"Is not the Nicene Creed a witness, in what it does not say, to the broader faith that must have been the religion of the century that adopted it?"[4]

Still, we need to understand how and why the early Church had no strong feelings on this topic for the first few hundred years, and why that changed so dramatically in later years.

One very simple reason that the earliest Christians had no dogmatic position on the afterlife is this: *They understood that the Scriptures were not clear on this subject.*

Today's Christians have no such latitude on this point. Most are convinced that the Scriptures are very clear on this doctrine of Hell and that anyone who refuses to see it their way is either a heretic, a fool, swayed by their emotions, or a victim of false teachers.

ONE VERY SIMPLE REASON THAT THE EARLIEST CHRISTIANS HAD NO DOGMATIC POSITION ON THE AFTERLIFE IS THIS: THEY UNDERSTOOD THAT THE SCRIPTURES WERE NOT CLEAR ON THIS SUBJECT.

But what if all three views were "Biblical"? What if all three views based their doctrine on the "clear teachings of Scripture"? What if they were only affirming certain verses in the Bible that conformed to their view and had developed elaborate explanations for why those other verses didn't teach what they appear to teach?

Well, I'm here to tell you, I think that all of those statements above are essentially true. Because, after looking at all three views, I can tell you that all three are certainly Biblical, (meaning they base their teaching on the Bible), and all three views assume to take a "clear teaching" approach when it comes to the verses that support their view (while arguing that opposing verses require more discernment to understand).

Obviously, either one of them is the correct view, or they are all wrong. But, they cannot all three be right. Hopefully we can all agree on these points.

So, I will fully admit that—whatever view you embrace—you must make a decision to accept a certain set of verses as authoritative and to dismiss another set. Neither of these three Christian views of Hell are iron-clad. Someone can always say, "But what about this verse?" and you will either have to explain why that verse isn't saying what it appears to say or admit that you don't know what it means, while you still hold tightly to the view you've decided to embrace.

To be fair, the Christian church took over 500 years to even attempt to divide over this teaching. The reasons why are self-evident: The Bible is of three minds on the question. However, one of those three views has a lot less convincing evidence than the other two.

In this book, I hope to show you the following:

- That the Eternal Suffering view has the weakest body of evidence

- That the other two views have stronger evidence

- That one of those last two views is more likely than the other

- That you don't need to agree with my conclusion

I mean that, by the way. This book is mainly concerned with demonstrating that the earliest Christians embraced Universal Reconciliation—which is very easy to do—and that the doctrine of Eternal Suffering is based on a misunderstanding of classic apocalyptic hyperbole.

Along the way we'll also look into the doctrine of Annihilation (or Conditional Immortality), the origins of all three doctrines, and what each view says about our idea of the nature and character of God.

That's just for starters. There's lots to cover. I hope you're ready for what's next.

CHAPTER 3

CONTRASTING VIEWS OF HELL

"For the wicked there are punishments, not perpetual, however, lest the immortality prepared for them should be a disadvantage, but they are to be purified for a brief period according to the amount of malice in their works. They shall therefore suffer punishment for a short space, but immortal blessedness having no end awaits them...the penalties to be inflicted for their many and grave sins are very far surpassed by the magnitude of the mercy to be showed to them."

—DIODORE OF TARSUS, (320 TO 394 A.D.)

As we've seen in the previous chapter, there have always been three views of Hell in the Christian Church. Before we go any further, let's take some time to examine each view and try to understand what each is all about.

ETERNAL SUFFERING

This is the view that most of us are most familiar with. If you're like me, you grew up being told that this is the "Christian" or "Biblical" view. You probably were not even taught that there were two other views at all. The only thing you needed to know was that "No one ever taught more about Hell than Jesus did" and "Those who die without Christ will suffer for an eternity separated from God in the lake of fire where the worm does not die and the fire is not quenched, etc."

In this view:

- God is too Holy to look upon our sins.

   "Your eyes are too pure to look on evil; you cannot tolerate wrongdoing." (Habbukuk 1:13)

- Our sins have separated us from God.

   "But your iniquities have separated you from your God; your sins have hidden his face from you, so that he will not hear." (Isaiah 59:2)

- Anyone who is not a Christian will suffer an endless eternal torment.

   "Then he [Jesus] will answer them, saying, 'Truly, I say to you, as you did not do it to one of the least of these, you did not do it to me.' And these will go away into eternal punishment, but the righteous into eternal life." (Mathew 25:41-46)

What Biblical texts support this view?
Matthew 25:41-46; Mark 9:43-48; 2 Thessalonians 1:9; Revelation 14:10-11; 19:20; 20:10-15.

Who believed this view?
Tertullian (160-220 A.D.), Augustine (354-430 A.D.), Thomas Aquinas (1225-1275 A.D.).

Summary

Because God is Holy, He cannot look on us because of our sins. Those who are washed in the blood of Christ are saved and make it into Heaven. Those without Christ remain covered in their sins and are doomed to an eternal separation from God in Hell where they will be tortured forever and ever.

Assumptions

Every human soul is eternal. Therefore, everyone will spend eternity in either Heaven or in Hell. Gehenna is the word for a place of eternal torment. When Jesus talks about "eternal punishment", he's talking about endless suffering that is equal in duration to the "eternal reward" of those who are in Christ.

> "Then he will say to those on his left, 'Depart from me, you cursed, into the eternal fire prepared for the devil and his angels. For I was hungry and you gave me no food, I was thirsty and you gave me no drink, I was a stranger and you did not welcome me, naked and you did not clothe me, sick and in prison and you did not visit me.' Then they also will answer, saying, 'Lord, when did we see you hungry or thirsty or a stranger or naked or sick or in prison, and did not minister to you?' Then he will answer them, saying, 'Truly, I say to you, as you did not do it to one of the least of these, you did not do it to me.' And these will go away into eternal punishment, but the righteous into eternal life." (Matthew 25:41-46)

ANNIHILATION (CONDITIONAL IMMORTALITY)

This view holds that those who die without Christ are doomed to a season of suffering in Hell until all their sins are atoned for, and then they will be destroyed forever and cease to exist.

In this view:

- Only God is Eternal.

  "[God] who alone has immortality, who dwells in unapproachable light, whom no one has ever seen or can see. To him be honor and eternal dominion." (1 Timothy 6:16)

- Eternal life must be granted to us by God.

  "...to those who by patience in well-doing seek for glory and honor and immortality, he will give eternal life. (Romans 2:7)

- Life is only found in Christ.

  "And this is the testimony, that God gave us eternal life, and this life is in his Son. Whoever has the Son has life; whoever does not have the Son of God does not have life." (1 John 5:11-12)

What other Biblical texts support this view?
Matthew 10:28; John 3:16; Romans 2:12; 1 Thessalonians 5:3; 2 Thessalonians 1:9; 2:8; 1 John 5:11-12; 1 Timothy 6:16.

Who believed this view?
Barnabus (70-130 A.D.), Mathetes (125-200 A.D.), Hermas (90-150 A.D.), Irenaeus (130-200 A.D.), and perhaps Justin Martyr (160 A.D.).

Summary
Because only God is eternal, those who are in Christ will receive eternal life, and those without Christ will be consumed in the fire after they have suffered for their sins in this life.

Assumptions

Human souls are not eternal by nature. Therefore, without God to sustain us, we will cease to exist. Most pronouncements about the fate of sinners use terms like *death, perish, destroy,* and other words that suggest the end of existence, not an eternal state of torment.

UNIVERSAL RECONCILIATION (OR PATRISTIC UNIVERSALISM)

This view holds that those who die without Christ will—like those who are in Christ—pass through the fire which is designed to purify, refine and restore everyone into right relationship with God. Eventually everyone will be redeemed and restored to a right relationship with God.

In this view:

- God is the savior of all mankind (not only believers)

  "For to this end we toil and strive, because we have our hope set on the living God, who is the Savior of all people, especially of those who believe." (1 Timothy 4:10)

- God has reconciled the whole world to Himself and no longer counts anyone's sins against them

  "…in Christ God was reconciling the world to himself, not counting their sins against them, and entrusting to us the message of reconciliation." (2 Cor. 5:19)

- God's punishments are intended to bring us into right relationship with Himself, not to destroy us.

  "For they [our earthly fathers] disciplined us for a short time as it seemed best to them, but he [God] disciplines us for our good, that we may share his holiness. For the moment all discipline seems painful rather than pleasant, but later it yields the peaceful fruit of righteousness to those who have been trained by it." (Hebrews 12:10-11)

What other Biblical texts support this view?

1 Timothy 4:10; 1 Corinthians 15:22; Ephesians 1:9-10; Romans 5:18-19; Colossians 1:19-20; Philippians 2:10-11.

Who believed this view?

Clement of Alexandria (150-215 AD), Origen (185-254 AD), Gregory of Nazianzus (329-390 AD), Gregory of Nysa (335-395 AD), Basil the Great (330-379 AD), Theophilus of Antioch (183 AD), Theodore of Mopsuestia (350-428 AD), Didymus the Blind (313-398 AD), Diodorus of Tarsus (390 AD), and numerous others.

Summary

God desires that everyone would be saved and none should perish. Since God alone has the power to redeem and restore everyone, God does so and thereby fulfills His desire through the finished work of Christ who came to reconcile the world to God. The punishment endured by the unrepentant in the afterlife is intended to correct and restore them into a right relationship with God.

Assumptions

God's will is that none should perish but that all come to the saving knowledge of Christ. God's love is eternal and His mercy and grace are everlasting. Therefore, God will do whatever it takes to woo and win every last human soul. In this way, God will eventually have the Universe align with His perfect will so that *"every knee will bow and every tongue will gladly confess that Jesus Christ is Lord to the glory of God, the Father."* (Phil. 2:10)

So, there we have a brief overview of all three views of Hell. Before we start to dig into each one, let's take some time to establish a few things first.

All three views of Hell agree that:

- Those who die without Christ will suffer in the afterlife

- Hell involves God's judgement of sin

- God's judgement will involve some form of fire

- The fire of Hell will not be a pleasant experience

So, no matter which view of Hell you may embrace, you do all agree on those points above. The reason I am taking the time to point this out is to respond to the misconception that Universalism does not involve the unrepentant sinner going to Hell, being judged in fire, or suffering for their sins. All three views share this in common.

The key differences between these three views of Hell is simply this: The duration and purpose of the suffering, and the nature and purpose of the fire.

THE KEY DIFFERENCES BETWEEN THESE THREE VIEWS OF HELL IS SIMPLY THIS: THE DURATION AND PURPOSE OF THE SUFFERING, AND THE NATURE AND PURPOSE OF THE FIRE.

This is what we'll cover in our next chapters. But, before we do, there are a few more things I'd like to point out here:

All three views of Hell also have this in common:

- They are based on numerous supporting Scriptures

- They were held by various early Christians

- They incorporate specific assumptions about God

- They assume certain things about the human soul

So, again, no matter which view of Hell you embrace, you do so because it's what you see the Bible affirming. You may also feel safe knowing that a certain handful of early Church Fathers or wise Christian teachers in the past once also held your views. Your view may also support your other convictions about the nature of God and the nature of human beings.

Once we can all agree on these things, I think it's safe to move forward and start to examine each of these three views in more detail.

Shall we?

CHAPTER 4

ETERNAL SUFFERING EXAMINED

"These, if they will, may go Christ's way, but if not let them go their way. In another place perhaps they shall be baptized with fire, that last baptism, which is not only painful, but enduring also; which eats up, as if it were hay, all defiled matter, and consumes all vanity and vice."

—GREGORY OF NAZIANZEU, BISHOP OF CONSTANTINOPLE. (330 TO 390 A.D.) ORACLES 39:19

In spite of what some pastors and Bible teachers would like you to believe, the Bible has very little to say about what happens to those who die without faith in Christ. In fact, it also has very little detail regarding what happens to those who die with faith in Christ either. Most of what we see in the Old Testament is only about the grave—literally "Sheol" or "Hades"—which is simply the place where everyone goes when they die.

> IF GOD'S PLAN ALL ALONG HAS BEEN TO TORTURE UNBELIEVERS IN HELL FOR ETERNITY, THEN WHY DIDN'T GOD BOTHER TO MENTION THIS FOR OVER 4,000 YEARS OF JEWISH HISTORY?

This fact alone begs the question: If God's plan all along has been to torture unbelievers in Hell for eternity, then why didn't God bother to mention this for over 4,000 years of Jewish history?

Wouldn't that be an important detail to address?

Other than one solitary reference in the Old Testament book of Daniel, there is not one reference in all of the Hebrew Scriptures that could be said to teach the doctrine of eternal torment for those who reject God's Law or refuse to worship Him.

Let's look at the Daniel reference:

> "Many of those who sleep in the dust of the ground will awake, these to everlasting life, but the others to disgrace and everlasting contempt." (Daniel 12:2)

If this verse was all you had to go on, would you assume that it was telling you anything about burning in an endless hell of eternal suffering? Hardly. Disgrace and contempt are certainly not enjoyable, but they are a far cry from burning forever and ever in endless torture.

Note: There is one other Old Testament reference in Isaiah 66, but we'll examine that one when we get into the New Testament references, since some of those are actually quoting that passage.

As author Steve Gregg notes:

> "Many Christians...believe that the traditional view of hell [eternal suffering] is one of the very pillars of the Christian faith, without which the death of Christ itself would be rendered meaningless. If this pillar is removed, or undermined, the whole gospel message, they feel, becomes destabilized, and in danger of collapse. Yet, when we delve into the scriptural teaching about hell, what we will find most striking is the infrequency of its being mentioned in Scripture. Hell, conceived as a place of future judgement, is not found in the Old Testament at all. This represents more than three-quarters of the Biblical material, covering a period of four thousand years of Divine revelation. What we find here is, essentially, silence."[1]

So, if the Old Testament scriptures say nothing about eternal suffering, and very little about annihilation or universal reconciliation, then where did these ideas come from?

Some will try to say that it was Jesus who introduced the idea of Hell—and in the New Testament scriptures it is true that Jesus does use a lot of language that appears to reference something close to what those who believe in eternal suffering describe, at least on the surface—but the idea of Hell, and specifically the concept of eternal suffering, did not originate with Jesus. It started in the Intertestamental Period—the period of time between the end of the Old Testament scriptures and the coming of Christ. Plus, the originators of the concept of Hell were not Jewish, and they were certainly not the followers of Jesus; they were pagans.

Specifically, the ideas of a paradise for the righteous separated by a gulf from the place of fire and torment where the unrighteous were tormented in flames, are all concepts found in the Talmud. But, the writers of the Talmud took these ideas from the Greeks and the Egyptians of their day, and these ideas were incorporated into other Jewish writings like 1 Enoch and the teachings of various Jewish rabbis at the time during the 400 year gap of time between the end of the Old Testament scriptures and the coming of Christ.

THEY ARE BASED ON VERY COMMON GREEK NOTIONS OF HADES AND ON PAGAN CONCEPTS OF THE AFTERLIFE WHICH CREPT INTO JEWISH THOUGHT AFTER THE OLD TESTAMENT WAS WRITTEN AND PRIOR TO THE COMING OF CHRIST.

What's important to note here is this: These ideas were never revealed by God to the Jewish people through their own Old Testament prophets. They are based on very common Greek notions of Hades and on pagan concepts of the afterlife which

crept into Jewish thought after the Old Testament was written
and prior to the coming of Christ.

This is exactly where the parable of Lazarus and the Rich
Man comes from; the same one that Jesus re-tells in the Gospels,
but with a slightly different spin. As numerous historians and
biblical scholars have noted time and again, this was an Egyptian
parable told, and often re-told, by many people around the time
of Christ[2]:

> "A doctoral dissertation at the University of Amsterdam identi-
> fied seven versions of the parable circulating in the first century.
> The fortunes of a rich man and a poor man are reversed in the
> afterlife. As often happens in the Bible, a preexisting story is
> adapted to present a [new] theological truth."[3]

And noted Biblical Scholar, N.T. Wright concurs:

> "The parable [of Lazarus and the Rich Man] is not, as often sup-
> posed, a description of the afterlife, warning people to be sure of
> their ultimate destination."[4]

So, because this parable of Lazarus and the Rich Man pre-
existed, it's highly unlikely that Jesus re-told it in order to affirm
the details of the afterlife found in the story. Rather, Jesus uses
this parable to teach a very poignant lesson about the dangers of
loving money rather than caring for people who are made in the
image of God.

Note that in the very same chapter where Jesus re-tells this
ancient parable, he starts by warning his disciples that they cannot serve both God and money, and this teaching offends the
Pharisees "who loved money" (v. 14). After this response, Jesus
tells the parable of Lazarus and the Rich Man.

To me, it is very significant that the concept of Hell as taught
by those who embrace eternal suffering is not found in the Old
Testament. Furthermore, it is very suspicious to me that the concepts incorporated into the doctrine came from non-biblical,

pagan sources that had infiltrated the Hebrew faith just prior to the coming of Christ.

Whether we like it or not, the doctrine of eternal suffering is part of the Christian faith today, and it seems as if almost everyone believes it.

As we've seen, there were even some early Christians who embraced the doctrine of eternal torment, although at the time they were in the minority.

So, what happened? Should we assume that the eventual rise of this view was due to the overwhelming amount of scriptural evidence? Or is there some other explanation for why universal reconciliation and annihilationism faded into the background as the concept of eternal suffering gained prominence?

First, let's examine the view itself and see what the doctrine is based on, biblically. Then we can deal with the question of how and why it gained popularity in the Christian Church after 500 A.D.

As noted earlier, the doctrine of eternal suffering is largely supported by these six verses of scripture:

- Matthew 25:41-46
- Mark 9:43-48
- 2 Thessalonians 1:9
- Revelation 14:10-11
- Revelation 19:20
- Revelation 20:10-15

There are other verses of course. But these are the main ones we will examine in this chapter to see what they teach and whether or not a strong case can be made for the doctrine.

We'll take one verse at a time.

MATTHEW 25:41-46

"Then he will say to those on his left, 'Depart from me, you cursed, into the eternal fire prepared for the devil and his angels. For I was hungry and you gave me no food, I was thirsty and you gave me no drink, I was a stranger and you did not welcome me, naked and you did not clothe me, sick and in prison and you did not visit me.' Then they also will answer, saying, 'Lord, when did we see you hungry or thirsty or a stranger or naked or sick or in prison, and did not minister to you?' Then he will answer them, saying, 'Truly, I say to you, as you did not do it to one of the least of these, you did not do it to me.' *And these will go away into eternal punishment, but the righteous into eternal life."* [emphasis mine]

The two verses that have the strongest weight in terms of eternal suffering are italicized for us above. Let's take the first one, verse 41, where Jesus himself says, *"Depart from me, you cursed, into the eternal fire prepared for the devil and his angels."*

Wow. Strong stuff, I'll admit. But notice that it is the fire that is eternal, not the people being cast into it. It's very possible for a mortal person to be tossed into an eternal fire. And that is exactly all we are told here in this verse. The quality of the fire they are tossed into is eternal. That is all the detail we are given.

Now, let's look at the final verse (46) where Jesus says: *"And these [the wicked] will go away into eternal punishment, but the righteous to eternal life."*

Much has been made about the fact that the word "eternal" here is used twice: Once to describe the punishment of the wicked, and again to describe the life of the righteous. The problem, many point out, is that if the duration of the punishment endured by the wicked is not endless, then neither can the duration of the life enjoyed by the righteous be endless.

Honestly, that's a very solid argument. We may do well to remember this sort of logic when we come to one of the verses that teaches universal reconciliation in an upcoming chapter. But I digress.

Is this true? Does the word "eternal" used to describe the suffering of the wicked, and the life of the righteous, mean an endless length of time? Not exactly.

The actual word in the Greek that is used here is "*aionios*" and while it may sometimes be used to suggest an endless duration of time, it is also quite often used in the scriptures to refer to "a very long time" that is not endless.

For example, in the Greek translation of the Old Testament, the Hebrew word "*olam*" is translated using the Greek word "*aionios*" in Isaiah 32-14-15 which says:

"The fortress will be abandoned, the noisy city deserted; citadel and watchtower will become a wasteland *forever* ["*aionios*"], the delight of donkeys, a pasture for flocks, *until the Spirit is poured on us from on high*, and the desert becomes a fertile field, and the fertile field seems like a forest." [emphasis mine]

Please notice that this verse tells us both that "*the fortress will… become a wasteland forever*" and that this will last "*until the Spirit is poured on us from on high.*" So, which is it? Will the fortress be a wasteland forever (without end)? Or will it only be a wasteland until the Spirit is poured out from on high? Obviously, it cannot be both. Therefore, the term "*aionios*" here does not mean "without end." It can only mean "for a very long time" which will come to an end when the Spirit is finally poured out.

This is not the only such example of the use of "*aionios*" in the Scriptures to refer to an indefinite period of time that is not necessarily endless in duration. And the same is true for the

Hebrew word "*olam*" which is also used over 300 times in the Old Testament scriptures to indicate something that endures for a very long time, but not necessarily without end. In at least twenty cases, the word "*olam*" is used to refer to events in the past. Therefore, "*olam*" and "*aionios*" are quite often used to refer to events that last a very long time, but are not necessarily without end.

According to the *Theological Word Book of the Old Testament*:

"The Septuagint generally translates both olam by aion which has essentially the same range of meaning. That neither the Hebrew nor the Greek word in itself contains the idea of endlessness is shown by the fact that they sometimes refer to events or conditions that occurred at a definite point in the past, and also by the fact that it is thought desirable to repeat a word, not merely saying "forever," but "forever and ever."...Both words came to be used to refer to a long age or period."[5]

And other scholars agree, noting that:

"Few are so bold as to claim that the Greek adjective 'aionios' always suggests 'infinity in time'—such thinking has been rejected by most modern exegetes."[6]

So, to circle back to the use of the term "*aionios*" in Matthew 25, it does not necessarily entail the meaning of "endless" in either use of the word; whether to refer to the duration of the punishment, or to the duration of the life. Frankly, it could be endless in one case, and nearly endless in the other.

Even Francis Chan, in his book *Erasing Hell* admitted that the meaning of the word "*aionios*" was not conclusive enough for him to say that Hell was indeed endless:

"The debate about hell's duration is much more complex than I first assumed. While I lean heavily on the side that says it is everlasting, I am not ready to claim that with complete certainty."[7]

What's going on here? Well, this is just one example of something you should get ready to notice a lot in the scriptures: *Hyperbole*. It's found literally everywhere in the Bible, and

OUR FAILURE TO GRASP THE FREQUENT USE OF HYPERBOLE IN THE BIBLE HAS LED TO MANY GRAVE MISUNDERSTANDINGS.

most especially from the mouth of Jesus. (And this statement is also an example of hyperbole, by the way.)

Our failure to grasp the frequent use of hyperbole in the Bible has led to many grave misunderstandings. This is nowhere more true than when it comes to the use of apocalyptic hyperbole in the Old Testament and when repeated by Jesus in the New Testament.

We'll talk more about this very soon.

For now, let's move on to the next verse that is used to support the doctrine of eternal suffering.

MARK 9:43-48

"If your hand causes you to stumble, cut it off. It is better for you to enter life maimed than with two hands to go into *hell, where the fire never goes out.* And if your foot causes you to stumble, cut it off. It is better for you to enter life crippled than to have two feet and *be thrown into hell.* And if your eye causes you to stumble, pluck it out. It is better for you to enter the kingdom of God with one eye than to have two eyes and *be thrown into hell, where 'the worms that eat them do not die, and the fire is not quenched.'"* [emphasis mine]

Once again, those English translators have taken the word "Gehenna" used by Jesus and placed the word "hell" here, which makes it very confusing for most of us to really understand.

As you may have noticed in our Introduction to this book, I called out the fact that the Old Testament prophet Jeremiah gave very similar prophetic warnings to the people in his day, using very similar terms.

However, when Jeremiah said those things, he was actually standing in the Valley of Hinnom or Gehenna. That's because "Gehenna" is an actual place just outside of Jerusalem where the Jewish people once sacrificed their own children to Molech by burning them on the altars. It's also the place where, after Jeremiah's prophecy about the destruction of Jerusalem came to pass, they stacked the dead bodies and burned them because there were too many to bury. (See Jeremiah 7:32-33; 19:6-9.)

In Mark 9:48 Jesus is actually quoting directly from the prophet Isaiah who is also using apocalyptic hyperbole to warn the Jewish people in his day of a very similar judgement that is coming upon them. Here Jesus is also referring to the very same place—Gehenna—which had become the garbage dump where they burned their trash. And, like what happened after Jeremiah's prophecy, Gehenna also became the place where the Romans piled dead bodies in 70 A.D. and burned them after they destroyed Jerusalem and the Temple as Jesus predicted they would.

IN OTHER WORDS, JESUS, JEREMIAH AND ISAIAH WERE WARNING THE JEWISH PEOPLE ABOUT A LITERAL DESTRUCTION THAT WAS COMING UPON THEM IN THEIR OWN LIFETIME. IT WAS NOT ABOUT AN EVENT THAT WOULD TAKE PLACE IN THE AFTERLIFE.

In other words, Jesus, Jeremiah and Isaiah were warning the Jewish people about a literal destruction that was coming upon them in their own lifetime. It was not about an event that would take place in the afterlife. It was a very real warning of a coming national judgement that actually resulted in their bodies being thrown into the Valley of Gehenna and burned up. Exactly as they had been warned.

Let's also take a moment to unpack the phrase used by both Jesus and Isaiah here:

> "...and be thrown into hell, where 'the worms that eat them do not die, and the fire is not quenched.'"

Now, just for the sake of argument, lets' say that Jesus was really speaking literally in this passage in Mark. If so, what does it tell us?

Well, if this is literal and not an example of apocalyptic hyperbole, then what Jesus is warning us about involves eternal worms and endless fire. However, this verse says nothing about eternal human beings in that fire who are alive to experience those immortal worms. In fact, to go back to the original reference from Isaiah, the people are not alive at all. They're dead:

> "And they shall go out and look on the dead bodies of the men who have rebelled against me. For their worm shall not die, their fire shall not be quenched, and they shall be an abhorrence to all flesh." (Isaiah 66:24)

Remember earlier where I mentioned the problems that occur when we misunderstand apocalyptic hyperbole? Well, this is a prime example of that.

All through the Old Testament scriptures, the prophets used apocalyptic hyperbole to warn against God's coming judgement. Quite often they would use phrases like the one above to overstate the absolute and total destruction that would come upon them if they refused to repent of their sins and return to God.

Here are a few other examples of apocalyptic hyperbole from the Old Testament. See if you can notice a few familiar phrases that get repeated by Jesus and other New Testament authors.

> "Behold, the Lord is riding on a swift cloud and comes to Egypt; and the idols of Egypt will tremble at his presence, and the heart of the Egyptians will melt within them." (Isaiah 19:1)

Isaiah prophesies against Babylon:

"For the stars of heaven and the constellations thereof shall not give their light: the sun shall be darkened in his going forth, and the moon shall not cause her light to shine. And I will punish the world for their evil, and the wicked for their iniquity; and I will cause the arrogancy of the proud to cease and will lay low the haughtiness of the terrible." (Isaiah 13:9-11)

Ezekiel prophesies against Egypt:

"And when I shall put thee [Pharaoh] out, I will cover the heaven, and make the stars thereof dark; I will cover the sun with a cloud, and the moon shall not give her light. All the bright lights of heaven will I make dark over thee, and set darkness upon thy land, saith the Lord God." (Ezekiel 30:18; 32:7-8)

Amos prophesies against Israel about how the Assyrians will destroy them:

"In that day, declares the Sovereign Lord, I will make the sun go down at noon and darken the earth in broad daylight" (Amos 8:9)

Isaiah prophesies against Edom:

"...Hearken, ye people: let the earth hear....All the host of heaven shall be dissolved, and the heavens shall be rolled together as a scroll....For my sword shall be satiated in heaven: behold it shall come down upon Edom, and upon the people of my curse, to judgment....For it is the day of the Lord's vengeance...its land will become burning pitch. It will not be quenched night or day; its smoke will go up forever." (Isaiah 34:1-10)

Notice anything? Did you see how these prophets pronounced a very real-world judgment against these people and yet used cosmic destruction language?

Notice how they each promise that the stars will go dark, or the heavens will be dissolved and rolled up like a scroll? Notice how they foretell that this destruction will be marked by the sun and moon not giving their light?

All of that? It's apocalyptic hyperbole: prophetic and poetic overstatements about the cosmic-level judgment that is about to come upon them all.

Poetic, not literal.

No stars were harmed in the destruction of Edom. No moons or suns were actually extinguished when Babylon and Egypt got sacked. No heavens were actually rolled into a taco in the Jerusalem sky.

This is hyperbole.

Now, go back and read what Jesus (and Isaiah) says about those who are *"thrown into Gehenna... where the worm does not die and the fire is not quenched."* If you do, you'll start to see how Jesus uses the exact same phrases to make his points. And when he does, the disciples understand that he is talking about a very real-world place (Gehenna) where their actual dead bodies would be tossed when the invading armies would surround Jerusalem and slaughter the innocent.

NO STARS WERE HARMED IN THE DESTRUCTION OF EDOM. NO MOONS OR SUNS WERE ACTUALLY EXTINGUISHED WHEN BABYLON AND EGYPT GOT SACKED. NO HEAVENS WERE ACTUALLY ROLLED INTO A TACO IN THE JERUSALEM SKY. THIS IS HYPERBOLE.

They knew—where we do not seem to—that this was very common Old Testament-style apocalyptic hyperbole used to communicate a very real warning of destruction and judgment that was about to come to pass.

The language is figurative, but the destruction is very, very real.

The point—and I do think I have made it—is that hyperbole is never literal, but the destruction always is. And, in addition to all of this, apocalyptic hyperbole never speaks of what happens to anyone after they die.

Finally, the context of Isaiah, chapters 60-66, references the coming of the Messiah, the destruction of the temple, and the inauguration of the New Covenant—all of which have already been fulfilled. As Steve Gregg demonstrates:

> "That these events have a first-century fulfillment was the view of the New Testament writers, who often quoted from this section, invariably applying its statements to their own times."[8]

He then goes on to provide examples:

- Isaiah 61:1-2 fulfilled in Luke 4:18

- Isaiah 61:11 fulfilled in Mark 4:28

- Isaiah 65:1-2 fulfilled in Romans 10:20-21

- Isaiah 65:13-14 fulfilled in Luke 6:20-25

- Isaiah 66:1-2 fulfilled in Acts 7:49-50

- Isaiah 66:20 fulfilled in Romans 15:16[9]

So, this passage in Isaiah 66:24 that Jesus quotes in Mark 9:43-48 is about an event which has already taken place in 70 AD, when the Jewish Temple was destroyed by the Romans. It's not about what happens to anyone's soul after they are dead.

Our next verse to examine is:

2 THESSALONIANS 1:9

> "*They will suffer the punishment of eternal destruction, away from the presence of the Lord and from the glory of his might…*" [emphasis mine]

The only thing eternal here is the destruction which the unrighteous suffer. In other words, their destruction is complete and final.

If we're honest, both this verse and the one above it are actually great verses to support the doctrine of Annihilation (or Conditional Immortality). Why? Because what they speak of are dead bodies eaten by eternal worms and burned by eternal fire, and people who suffer "eternal destruction"—not eternal conscious torment.

And, if we keep in mind what we've already learned about how the terms "*aionios*" (eternal) and "apocalyptic hyperbole" are often used in the Bible regarding warnings of destruction, we are probably safe to assume that—whatever this verse might mean—chances are pretty good that it probably doesn't speak of something that is literally endless.

The next three verses we're going to examine all come from the book of Revelation. So, before we dig into those, let's stop and talk about this book first.

Revelation is the single most misunderstood and confusing book in the entire Bible. It would be hard to say that anyone understands it completely. Most of the time our misunderstandings come from not recognizing apocalyptic hyperbole when we see it. However, many misunderstandings come from the various assumptions most readers bring with them into the text.

For example: Most assume that the book is about some far-future events that have yet to take place. This is frankly not the case. Revelation is a very detailed and metaphorical account of the destruction of Jerusalem in 70 AD by the Romans. It is filled with symbolism and hyperbole and draws heavily from the Old Testament prophets, employing the very same apocalyptic terminology common to that literature.

The purpose of Revelation is to prophetically critique the Roman Empire. As author Brian Zahnd tells us:

> "Revelation is a daring proclamation that Jesus Christ, not Julius Caesar or any other emperor, is the world's true emperor and

Savior. [It is] a wild and creative portrayal of the clash between the beastly empire of Rome and the peaceable reign of the Lamb of God. What Revelation portrays in powerful symbol is the triumph of Christ and His Kingdom....The only way to consistently interpret the book of Revelation is to acknowledge that everything is communicated as a symbol."[10]

So, as long as we're starting from the same place, let's take a look at these next three verses that appear to support endless suffering from this wildly misunderstood book:

REVELATION 14:9-11

"And another angel, a third, followed them, saying with a loud voice, "If anyone worships the beast and its image and receives a mark on his forehead or on his hand, he also will drink the wine of God's wrath, poured full strength into the cup of his anger, and *he will be tormented with fire and sulfur in the presence of the holy angels and in the presence of the Lamb. And the smoke of their torment goes up forever and ever, and they have no rest, day or night*, these worshipers of the beast and its image, and whoever receives the mark of its name." [emphasis mine]

There is so much to unpack here. I hope you're ready.

First, let's keep in mind that this passage is referring specifically to anyone who *"worships the beast and its image and receives the mark on his forehead or on his hand."* This warning is not given to everyone who dies apart from Christ. It is directed at anyone who—during the time that the Beast reigns—takes the fabled "Mark of the Beast" and worships him.

Now, one thing I think we should understand here is that the Beast is Nero and that the "Mark of the Beast" was related to the number of his name. How do we know this? Here's how:

"Let him who has understanding calculate the number of the beast, for the number is that of a man; and his number is six hundred and sixty-six." (Rev. 13:18)

The Hebrew spelling of "Nero Caesar" was NRWN QSR. Since Hebrew letters doubled as numbers it was a simple thing to take that name and add them together which adds up exactly to 666. (Example: N = 50 R = 200 W = 6 N =50 Q = 100 S = 60 R = 200)

One fascinating variant of this same passage notes that some manuscripts read: 616 rather than 666. Why is that? Because when Revelation was later copied into Latin the name Nero Caesar didn't add up to 666, it added up to 616. So, to make it easier for those later Latin-speaking (non-Hebrew reading) Christians to arrive at the same conclusion the number was changed to 616 in certain translations.

Want more proof? Ok, in Revelation 17:9-10 John tells us:

> "Here is the mind which has wisdom. The seven heads are seven mountains on which the woman sits, and they are seven kings; five have fallen, one is, the other has not yet come; and when he comes, he must remain a little while."

You've probably heard that the "seven mountains" correspond to the seven hills of Rome. However, did you know that the seven kings also point to Nero as the Beast? They do. Because John tells us that: "Five have fallen, one is, the other has not yet come and when he comes, he must remain a little while." And here's why that matters: According to Josephus, the Roman historian, Julius Caesar was the first king, followed by August, Tiberius, Caligula and Claudius. The sixth king? That was Nero. So, he is the "one (who) is."

The seventh king—the one who followed Nero—was Galba, and, as John prophesied, he reigned for a short time (about seven months).

Nero, as the sixth king of Rome, was the first to persecute Christians in the First Century. He started persecuting them in November of 64 AD and ended on June 8, 68 AD when he killed himself. That was *forty-two* months of persecution. Notice what John says about the Beast:

> "And there was given to him a mouth speaking arrogant words and blasphemies; and authority to act for *forty-two months* was given him." (Rev. 13:5)

Coincidence? I think not. Clearly John is going out of his way to let his readers know that "The Beast" had a name that, in the Hebrew, added up to a number (666) and that he was the sixth and current king of Rome, and that his persecution would last exactly forty-two months. What could be more clear than this?

Need more proof? Ok, Nero was also called "The Beast" by contemporary pagan writer Apollinius of Tyana, who said of Nero:

> "In my travels…I have seen many wild beasts of Arabia and India; but this beast, that is commonly called a Tyrant, I know not how many heads it has, nor if it be crooked of claw, and armed with horrible fangs…. And of wild beasts you cannot say that they were ever known to eat their own mother, but Nero gorged himself on this diet."

Note that Nero murdered his own parents and his brother, and his pregnant wife, in addition to several other family members. We also have evidence from the Romans that Nero enjoyed dressing up as a wild beast and raping male and female prisoners.

Still not convinced? Consider that all of the earliest Church Fathers from Irenaeus in the first century, all the way through to St. Beatus in the 8th century agreed that "The Beast" was Nero.

That's where I'll stop. But, at least to me, it's fairly obvious that the "Beast" was Nero. So, if we go back to Rev. 14:9-11, what we're told is that anyone who specifically took the mark of Nero on their forehead or hand, or who worshipped Nero, would be:

"...tormented with fire and sulfur in the presence of the holy angels and in the presence of the Lamb. And the smoke of their torment goes up forever and ever, and they have no rest, day or night..."

So, this verse is not helpful to those want to use it to teach that everyone who dies without Christ will suffer a similar fate as these people. However, I'd still like to suggest that even these who took the Mark of Nero did not suffer anything literally like this in the afterlife. Here's why:

Remember a few pages back when we talked about apocalyptic hyperbole and how New Testament prophets tended to use very similar language? Well, this is another example of that. In this passage, John borrows language from Isaiah 34:10, which says:

"Night and day it shall not be quenched; its smoke shall go up forever. From generation to generation it shall lie waste; none shall pass through it forever and ever."

As a reminder, this is the chapter where Isaiah was prophesying against Edom. He's using apocalyptic hyperbole. It's not meant to be taken literally. But, don't take my word for it. Just travel to where Edom used to be. That would be the modern-day nation of Jordan. If you go there you won't see an eternal column of smoke going up into the sky forever. You'll also not be prevented from passing through the area by any supernatural forces. That's because this verse in Isaiah is not meant to be taken literally. It's hyperbole.

So, if Isaiah didn't mean for this statement about eternally-rising smoke to be taken literally, maybe we shouldn't take the quotation of Isaiah here in Revelation to be about something literal either.

One last part of the verse in Revelation 14 that I want to look at is this:

"…and they have no rest, day or night…"

Now, we may be tempted to think that this phrase is saying that the wicked will suffer endlessly and this is why they have no rest, day or night. But that's not what the verse is referring to. Not at all.

This phrase is a reference to God's Sabbath rest. As the author of Hebrews notes:

"Therefore, as the Holy Spirit says,

"Today, if you hear his voice,
do not harden your hearts as in the rebellion,
     on the day of testing in the wilderness,
where your fathers put me to the test
     and saw my works for forty years.
Therefore I was provoked with that generation,
and said, 'They always go astray in their heart;
     they have not known my ways.'
As I swore in my wrath,
     'They shall not enter my rest.'" (Hebrews 3:7-11)

And then, later in the next chapter we read this:

"*So then, there remains a Sabbath rest for the people of God, for whoever has entered God's rest has also rested from his works as God did from his.*

Let us therefore strive to enter that rest, so that no one may fall by the same sort of disobedience." (Hebrews 4:9-11)

This is the "rest" that is in view in the Revelation passage. The point is that those who take the mark of the Beast will "have no rest, day or night," because they are cut off from the promised Sabbath Rest that God promised to His people.

This is also exactly the same sort of "rest" that Jesus references when he says:

"Come to me, all who labor and are heavy laden, and I will give you rest." (Matthew 11:28)

This rest that Jesus promises those who follow him is not just any ordinary rest. Not at all. It's specifically the promised Sabbath rest that the author of Hebrews speaks of, and it's also the same Sabbath rest that the worshippers of Nero (the Beast) will not receive, day or night.

So, the point of that phrase is not that these people will be suffering without any rest from their suffering. The point is that those who take the mark of Nero will be in danger of forfeiting the Sabbath rest of God.

Therefore, the passage is not telling us about the duration of the suffering, or about literal eternal smoke, or about what everyone who dies without Christ will suffer. If anything, it's another example of apocalyptic hyperbole that is not intended to be taken literally—certainly not in regards to the eternal smoke or fire—and should not be used to teach anything about the afterlife for those born after the reign of Nero.

Next, let's look at the second verse from Revelation:

REVELATION 19:19-21

> "And I saw the beast and the kings of the earth with their armies gathered to make war against him who was sitting on the horse and against his army. And the beast was captured, and with it the false prophet who in its presence had done the signs by which he deceived those who had received the mark of the beast and those who worshiped its image. These two were thrown alive into the lake of fire that burns with sulfur. And the rest were slain by the sword that came from the mouth of him who was sitting on the horse, and all the birds were gorged with their flesh."

If you're tracking with me so far, you can probably guess what I'm going to point out in this passage. First, that it is not all mankind that we see cast "alive into the lake of fire that burns with sulfur," it is specifically and only Nero (the Beast) and the False Prophet who receive this sentence.

Also, if we note that "these two are thrown alive into the lake of fire" it is significant that "the rest were slain" and this means, they were not alive, but dead. So, even if Nero and the False Prophet were actually thrown alive into the lake of fire, what we see is that everyone else is first killed and then "all the birds gorged on their flesh." (And this image of birds gorging on the flesh of the slain is yet another apocalyptic hyperbole referenced from Jeremiah 7:33; 19:7; and 34:20.)

AGAIN, WE CAN TELL FROM THE EXTREME SPECIFICITY OF THIS VERSE THAT THE PASSAGE SAYS ABSOLUTELY NOTHING ABOUT THE FATE OF THOSE WHO DIE APART FROM CHRIST.

Again, we can tell from the extreme specificity of this verse that the passage says absolutely nothing about the fate of those who die apart from Christ. What we do know is that this is a highly metaphorical verse which, if anything, refers to those who worshipped Nero, and took the mark of the Beast. And what is in view here is the literal destruction they suffered in AD 70, not in the afterlife.

The next verse does pose a few more problems, however. Let's take a look.

REVELATION 20:10-15

> "...and the devil who had deceived them was thrown into the lake of fire and sulfur where the beast and the false prophet were, and they will be tormented day and night forever and ever.

> "Then I saw a great white throne and him who was seated on it. From his presence earth and sky fled away, and no place was found for them. And I saw the dead, great and small, standing before the throne, and books were opened. Then another book

was opened, which is the book of life. And the dead were judged by what was written in the books, according to what they had done. And the sea gave up the dead who were in it, Death and Hades gave up the dead who were in them, and they were judged, each one of them, according to what they had done. Then Death and Hades were thrown into the lake of fire. This is the second death, the lake of fire. *And if anyone's name was not found written in the book of life, he was thrown into the lake of fire.*"

Ok, there's a lot here. So, let's try to take these verses one at a time.

First, we have a statement about how the Devil, the Beast and the False Prophet are thrown into lake of fire. That's not really a problem for us since we are not any of those people. Perhaps Nero (the Beast) was thrown into the lake of fire, and the False Prophet, and if there is a personal, literal Devil, or Satan, then he is there, too.

But this doesn't tell us what will happen to the rest of us. These three are apparently "tormented day and night forever and ever," which sounds bad, but, as we've already seen, the use of "*aionios*" or the phrase "forever and ever" does not necessarily mean "without end."

The next part gets a bit more interesting. This is where all the dead are judged at the great white throne of God. This would be about you, me, and everyone who has ever lived.

The first thing we note is that, in the presence of the One who sits upon this great white throne, all earth and sky vanish away. What's up with that? No earth? No sky? Ok, then.

Next we see "the dead, both great and small, standing before the throne and books were opened." What books are these? We are not told. Interestingly enough, this entire passage is only about the dead. What happens to the living? That's sort of what we find out in the next chapter of Revelation. Keep that in mind as we continue.

Then, *"another book was opened, which is the book of life."* This book is certainly more significant than those other books. We'll see why in a moment.

But, next "...*the dead were judged by what was written in the books, according to what they had done."* This is where all of the books—the book of life and those other unnamed books—come into play. The dead are judged by what was written in those books.

Finally, more dead people show up from a few other places: *"the sea gave up the dead who were in it, Death and Hades gave up the dead who were in them, and they were judged, each one of them, according to what they had done."* Notice that we started with all the dead being judged by those books, and then we had the sea give up its dead—even though there is no longer any sky or earth—and then "Death and Hades" gave up their dead. So, apparently, there are several places where the dead are taken from and brought before the great white throne to be judged by what was written in these books.

One reason for parsing out the dead in the earth and the dead in the sea is explained by David Bentley Hart in his notation for this verse in his own translation of the New Testament:

> "It was a common belief in antiquity, shared by pagans and Jews alike, that the souls of those who die on earth descend to Hades, but the souls of those who perish at sea descend to a place below the waters, or wander the waves as ghosts."[11]

So, this passage is incorporating ancient mythology about the fate of the dead as both Jewish and pagan folklore would have accepted it. But, almost no one today accepts such primitive notions about where the dead go who are buried on land compared to where the dead go who are buried at sea. And yet, we seem to have no problem accepting this passage as literally true—as if the dead in the sea are somehow being kept in a different location than the rest of the dead who are in Hades, or some other place in the depths of the earth.

Keep in mind that the author of Revelation is writing a highly symbolic account of some very real-world events and does so by incorporating primitive folklore about the dead that no one today would reasonably accept. This begs the question: If we do not believe—as the first century readers would have—that there are two separate holding areas for the dead depending on whether they die at sea or on land, then why would we accept that what John is describing in this verse is literally what will happen to the dead? In other words, if John isn't right about this notion of the dead at sea being held separately from the rest of the dead, then why would we assume the rest of what he's telling us is necessarily true in the literal sense? Apparently, in this verse John is confused by his own primitive assumptions about the dead at sea and the dead on the earth. He incorporates his superstition into this text about the great white throne judgement. Should we blindly accept his strange notion about what happens to those who die at sea as part of what is apparently taking place in this passage?

I don't want us to dwell too much on this point, but it does allow us to see where John's personal assumptions—and those of his readers—are imported into the text and how these ideas interact with everything else that is being communicated here.

So, let's get back to the original verse and look at this last part:

"...Death and Hades were thrown into the lake of fire. This is the second death, the lake of fire. And if anyone's name was not found written in the book of life, he was thrown into the lake of fire."

There's a lot going on here. First, both Death and Hades—which have already given up their dead to be judged by God—are themselves thrown into the lake of fire. That means that, after this event, there is no longer any place called Death or Hades. These places have now been burned up in the lake of fire. Please keep this in mind, because, after we look at the next chapter of Revelation, we'll want to come back to this important detail.

Finally, we are left with the most ominous sentence of all: *"… if anyone's name was not found in the book of life, he was thrown into the lake of fire."*

That may be the mic-drop moment for those who believe in the doctrine of eternal suffering. But, I would ask you to notice that it does not tell us that there *were* any whose names were not found in the book of life, nor do we see any such people being cast into the lake of fire during or after this great white throne judgment.

In other words: This is an "if/then" statement, but beyond this we are not told, or shown, whether there are any who meet the "if" side of the statement.

Maybe you would say that this is simply me splitting hairs, but I would suggest to you that we are given such a hair and we are being invited to split it, based on the way this passage is written. If the author had wanted there to be no wiggle room, then I submit that none would have been offered. Yet, I would argue, we are handed at least a small amount of wiggle room here, and I would gladly accept it as a measure of God's grace, no matter how small.

What's more, I think if we continue on to read the next chapter, we might notice that these events do not seem to be talking about future events at all, but about events which have already taken place, or are already playing out here and now.

Now, the earth and the sky and the sea have not literally ceased to exist. So, if this is literal then clearly none of this has happened yet. But, if some of this has happened—and I do believe I can show you where quite a bit of it has indeed already happened—then I believe we really need to rethink the entire thing.

So, let's look at Revelation 21 and see if we can find any clues about whether these events are still to come, or if they are already in motion. This may take some time to unpack, but I think it's key to really understanding what's happening at the end of Revelation 19, since the two events are so closely related to one another.

Revelations 21 begins like this:

"Then I saw a new heaven and a new earth, for the first heaven and the first earth had passed away, and the sea was no more. And I saw the holy city, New Jerusalem, coming down out of heaven from God, prepared as a bride adorned for her husband. And I heard a loud voice from the throne saying, "Behold, the dwelling place of God is with man. He will dwell with them, and they will be his people, and God himself will be with them as their God." (Rev. 21:1-3)

John kicks off this chapter by declaring that the "New Jerusalem"—which is the Bride of Christ—has come down from heaven in fulfillment of the promise that "the dwelling place of God" would be "with man" and that God "will dwell with them, and they will be his people, and God himself will be with them as their God." (Rev. 21:3)

I know that many are tempted to read this passage—and certainly this entire epistle of John—as if it were entirely futuristic. But there are some problems with that, I think. Especially when it comes to the New Covenant, which the prophet Jeremiah foreshadowed, and Jesus proclaimed as being inaugurated on the night before his crucifixion at the final Passover supper with his disciples, saying: *"This cup is the New Covenant in my blood."*

As a reminder, the New Covenant is simply this:

"For this is the covenant that I will make with the house of Israel after those days, declares the Lord: I will put my laws into their minds, and write them on their hearts, and I will be their God, and they shall be my people." (Hebrews 8:10)

Keep in mind, the old city of Jerusalem which existed at the time of Christ, and before John wrote Revelation, was destroyed in AD 70. Its destruction signaled the "end of the age", and the entire Old Covenant system ended with it.

Out of the ashes of that temporal city arose the new spiritual Jerusalem, and with the destruction of that Old Covenant Temple there was constructed a new, living Temple of the New Covenant, which is the Church; The Bride of Christ.

Later in this same chapter, John says:

"Then came one of the seven angels who…spoke to me, saying, 'Come, I will show you the Bride, the wife of the Lamb." And he carried me away in the Spirit to a great high mountain and showed me the holy city Jerusalem coming down out of heaven from God, having the glory of God…" (Rev. 21:9-11)

So, we know that the Church is the Bride of Christ, and, as John tells us in Revelation, "New Jerusalem" has already come down from Heaven—by the power of the indwelling Holy Spirit—and begins to grow, to cover the entire earth.

Then John goes on to say:

"And I saw no temple in the city, for its temple is the Lord God the Almighty and the Lamb. And the city has no need of sun or moon to shine on it, for the glory of God gives it light, and its lamp is the Lamb. By its light will the nations walk, and the kings of the earth will bring their glory into it, and her gates will never be shut by day—and there will be no night there. They will bring into it the glory and the honor of the nations. But nothing unclean will ever enter it, nor anyone who does what is detestable or false, but only those who are written in the Lamb's book of life." (Rev. 21:22-27)

Within the Church—or "New Jerusalem"—there is no temple other than Jesus Himself. He abides within us, and we abide within Him. We are the living Temple of the Holy Spirit where Christ lives, and Christ is the living Temple where all of us "live and move and have our being." (Acts 17:28)

Christ is our light, and because of this, we are the light of the world. As Jesus already told us: "You are the light of the world—like a city on a hilltop that cannot be hidden." (Matt. 5:14)

So, the Bride of Christ is here now. We are the Incarnation of Christ in the world today. He is our Head, and we are His Body.

Now, let's go back and re-read that first part of this chapter:

"And I heard a loud voice from the throne saying, "Behold, the dwelling place of God is with man. He will dwell with them, and they will be his people, and God himself will be with them as their God." (Rev. 21:3)

Has God not already made His dwelling among men? Isn't this what Jesus and the Apostles proclaimed over and over again? Has God not *already* made his dwelling with mankind? Isn't the promise of the New Covenant awfully similar to what we read in this verse?

The "New Jerusalem" has already been planted like a seed on the earth. It continues to grow, and the Lord is adding to

THE "NEW JERUSALEM" HAS ALREADY BEEN PLANTED LIKE A SEED ON THE EARTH. IT CONTINUES TO GROW, AND THE LORD IS ADDING TO HER NUMBER DAILY AS HIS KINGDOM ADVANCES AND HIS RULE AND REIGN EXPANDS.

Her number daily as His Kingdom advances and His rule and reign expands.

So, let's go back and retrace our steps: At the end of Revelation 20, there is a great white throne judgment. The dead (and only the dead) are judged according to what is written in the book of life. The earth and the sky and sea cease to exist. Then, both Death and Hades (where the dead were once kept in prison), are thrown into the lake of fire. After this, we see a new heaven and a new earth, and then a new Jerusalem comes down out of heaven and the Bride of Christ is revealed.

Do you see it? These events have already happened. This judgment of the dead took place when Christ descended into Hades (the grave), preached to the souls held captive there, and then led them all into paradise when he resurrected.

As one Christian historian tells us:

"In the early ages of the church great stress was laid on 1 Peter 3:19: "He (Christ) went and preached unto the spirits in prison.".…"It was believed that our Lord not only proclaimed his Gospel to all the dead, but that he liberated them all."[12]

But, I can hear you asking, "What about the earth and the sky and the sea vanishing away?"

That's a great question, and for the answer I will appeal to New Testament scholar, Gregory K. Beale.

A few years ago I interviewed Dr. Beale about his book *The Temple and the Church's Mission* and he said that he had noticed something as he was writing a commentary of the book of Revelation for the New International Greek Testament Commentary series. Here's what he found:

"As I was near the end of finishing the book I was looking at the last vision from the book of Revelation [Chapter 20] and as I finished studying that section I saw that John said, "I saw the new heavens and the new earth and the old heavens and earth have passed away and were no more and there was no more any sea" and the rest of the vision doesn't appear to talk about a new creation. It speaks of what's envisioned as a city in the shape of the Holy of Holies that is garden-like.

The way to simply solve this is that John sees this vision of the new heavens and the new earth and then he focuses in on a particular location which is the New Jerusalem, or the city itself, shaped like the Holy of Holies that is garden-like. That's one possible understanding. But, in fact, from a number of considerations exegetically from chapters 21 and 22 of Revelation it is apparent that the reason John doesn't go on to describe the undulating valleys and rivers is because in fact he is equating the new heavens and the new earth with the City, the new Jerusalem.

So, then the question arises once we are convinced of that, is "Why is that?" I mean, it's very odd. You can maybe picture a Star Trek episode where they find a planet that is square and is garden-like but it's a very weird picture. So, in the commentary I actually had a two-page explanation of what I thought was going on. Of course, part of the solution is to see that the Garden of Eden was a temple of God's presence and Adam was the first priest and he should have faithfully spread the boundaries of God's presence until the Garden covered the entire earth. Of course, that immediately answers the question of why the new heavens and the new earth is equated with a garden (in Revelation). Because now Eden has finally become co-equal with the New Heavens and the New Earth."[13]

Hopefully you can follow what Dr. Beale is saying here. The terms for heaven and earth were often equated throughout scripture with the Garden of Eden and the Temple of God. So, when John refers to the "New Heavens and the New Earth" in

Revelation 21, he starts to describe a new Temple, which is the Bride of Christ; which is us, the Church.

WHEN JOHN REFERS TO THE "NEW HEAVENS AND THE NEW EARTH" IN REVELATION 21, HE STARTS TO DESCRIBE A NEW TEMPLE, WHICH IS THE BRIDE OF CHRIST; WHICH IS US, THE CHURCH.

This means the old earth and old heaven—literally the Old Covenant Temple and the Law—have been destroyed and have vanished away. Now, God is making all things new. That is what was inaugurated at the Lord's Supper when Jesus declared the New Covenant with us, and what has been in motion ever since.

Dr. Beale also goes on to explain further:

"What it means is that where we're standing now in God's redemptive, historical program is that we're part of the end times Temple, and it's a literal Temple. The literal, again according to Hebrews, is not always the physical. In this case the physical has always pointed towards God's presence with His people. So, Christ is the Tabernacle-ing Temple in John 1 and his resurrection continues that Temple. And so the point of the Temple…is to show that this Temple is to be expanded. The way that occurs in the New Testament is through believers being made in the image of God. What do you do with images? The same thing that happened with Adam in Genesis. He's made in the image of God and you put him in the Temple, which is the Garden of Eden. So, when we become believers we become part of the Temple of God but we're images in the Temple to reflect Him. If that is the case, then as we go out into the World, whether through the testimony of Word or Life, we're to spread the presence of God. As people come to faith through our life or word, or both, basically what's happening is that this is the Temple expanding. God's presence expands outward from us, through us, to others."[14]

So, there is very strong evidence that these chapters in Revelation are not at all talking about some future end-of-the-world event that has yet to occur. Instead, what we're reading here is a very highly allegorical and symbolic description of the spiritual realities that have transpired due to the coming of Christ, his death on the cross, his descent into Hades to preach the Gospel to the dead there, his resurrection which emptied Death and Hades, and the coming of the "New Heaven and the New Earth" which are signs of the birth of the "New Jerusalem"—the Bride of Christ, or the Church.

Therefore, nothing that is being described in these chapters has anything to do with what happens to anyone after they are dead. All of this, especially Revelation 20 through 21, is a veiled, symbolic description of the triumph of Christ over death. It's a picture of the end of one age and the beginning a glorious new creation that we are already grafted into.

Now, we're already halfway through Revelation 21, and it's very tempting to keep moving forward here because there are some very amazing ideas to explore, especially when it comes to the doctrine of Universal Reconciliation. But, for now, let's stop here and take a breath.

What have we learned so far?

Most of the texts that appear to teach the doctrine of eternal suffering are not about what happens to souls after they die without faith in Christ. Many are either describing very literal events related to the national judgment of Israel in 70 AD, or refer to spiritual events that have already taken place at the coming of Christ, or take pre-existing parables too literally and miss the original point about the importance of caring for the poor.

Even more intriguing is the idea that what we read in Revelation 20 may actually be about events that have already taken place in the past. If so, then what we read about Death and Hades being emptied and then thrown into the lake of fire to be destroyed is very interesting. Could John be suggesting that Hades (or Hell) itself has now been made obsolete in view of Christ's death and resurrection?

That question will have to wait for now. But we will return to it later.

One thing is certain: What we do *not* see in any of these texts are warnings for those who do not have faith in Christ to repent or suffer eternally in an endless hell of fire and torment. We see apocalyptic hyperbole being misread as literal. We see warnings about destruction and death for those who are not in Christ, prior to 70 AD. But we still see no explicit statements about the eternal suffering of the unrighteous.

But there are still questions to be answered about this doctrine before we're done. For example, one thing we haven't really explored yet is the question of whether the doctrine of Eternal Suffering lines up with the character and nature of God, especially as revealed to us by Christ.

We're going to take some time to cover that in our next chapter.

CHAPTER 5

IS GOD A MONSTER?

"The Word seems to me to lay down the doctrine of the perfect obliteration of wickedness, for if God shall be in all things that are, obviously wickedness shall not be in them. For it is necessary that at some time evil should be removed utterly and entirely from the realm of being."

—ST. MACRINA THE BLESSED, (330 TO 379 A.D.)

As we've already mentioned, the Old Testament scriptures do not teach anything about an eternal hell of suffering for the wicked. This in itself is a very important fact that we should take into account when evaluating this doctrine.

If this was God's plan all along, then why didn't He mention this all-important fate of the unrighteous to Adam, or Abraham, or Moses, or Daniel, or Ezekiel, or Isaiah, or Jeremiah, or David?

Why keep this a secret until—presumably—Jesus arrives on the scene?

We've already talked about how this teaching originated in the period of time between the end of the Old Testament and the coming of Christ.

The Greeks and the Egyptians at the time of Christ had already started to introduce these concepts into Jewish thought long before Jesus was born. Eventually, the Jewish rabbis and teachers of the Law began to incorporate these ideas of endless punishment for the wicked into their teachings. But, as we've pointed out, none of this came from inspired sources. Instead, this was something new that had crept into Jewish thought over time.

Because of this, we know that this was the popular view of many Jewish teachers at the time of Christ. But, does this mean that Jesus also accepted this view?

This is a crucial question for us to answer. If we hope to understand what Jesus meant when he talked about "Gehenna" or "Hell," we need to first determine what side of this argument he stood on.

To put it another way:

"Biblical scholarship usually commends the practice of reading passages in the light of their historical settings and circumstances. But which historical precedent should inform our understanding of Jesus' use of Gehenna—the rabbinic usage current in His time, or that of the canonical prophets? Commentators often assume without question that Jesus accepted the rabbinic convention in His use of Gehenna, rather than following the precedent found in the Old Testament. We have already noted that John [the Baptist] borrowed from Jeremiah's imagery in warning of the impending judgment. What would be more natural than for Jesus to do the same?"[1]

"The Valley of Hinnom [Gehenna] had one significance to Jeremiah and Isaiah, and a very different one to the rabbis of Christ's day. *In seeking to identify the backstory behind Christ's use of Gehenna, our choice must weigh the respective likelihood of Christ taking His verbal cues from the Pharisees, on the one hand, or from the Prophets, on the other.*"[2] [emphasis mine]

This, for me, is the most significant question for us to answer when it comes to this idea of eternal suffering. Do we really believe that Jesus would have embraced an idea that was not found in the Old Testament scriptures, that was not taught by the Old Testament prophets, but was introduced afterwards by pagan philosophers and poets?

Or, to put it another way: Do we actually think that Jesus would have sided with the Pharisees on this issue, knowing that there was no basis for such a doctrine in the entire Jewish history?

DO WE REALLY BELIEVE THAT JESUS WOULD HAVE EMBRACED AN IDEA THAT WAS NOT FOUND IN THE OLD TESTAMENT SCRIPTURES, THAT WAS NOT TAUGHT BY THE OLD TESTAMENT PROPHETS, BUT WAS INTRODUCED AFTERWARDS BY PAGAN PHILOSOPHERS AND POETS?

That, to me, is a bridge too far. Not only can I *not* imagine Jesus agreeing with the Pagan poets and philosophers on this point, I cannot fathom that Jesus would agree with the Pharisees on this doctrine either. Not just because they were the religious leaders of the day who opposed his teaching and rejected his Messianic ministry, but simply because their ideas about God were in direct conflict with the image of God as revealed by Jesus.

From the beginning, Jesus challenged the notion that God played favorites. In his Sermon on the Mount, Jesus tells us that God brings rain on the just and on the unjust. This is in direct contradiction to what Moses had taught them about God's disposition toward the wicked. (See Deut. 28:1-24)

In fact, Jesus tells his disciples to turn the other cheek and to love their enemies specifically because this is what God does to His own enemies. So, when we love our enemies, we are like God who sends the rain on the righteous and the unrighteous alike. (See Matt. 5:45)

Jesus also shows us an "Abba" who, like the father of the prodigal son, goes out of his way to seek out his children; to embrace them, forgive them, and extend mercy to them, and who does not require punishment before extending this love to us.

Taking these facts into account, I find it highly unlikely that Jesus would have accepted the new teaching of Eternal Suffering, as the Pharisees had done. It seems far outside of his character to have embraced such a doctrine, especially in light of the merciful, patient, and loving God he revealed to us.

Let's also take a moment to look at some of the assumptions made by those who accept this doctrine of Eternal Suffering and see if these concepts are actually supported by the scriptures.

Because God is Holy, He cannot even look on us because of our sins. This separates us from God, and therefore, anyone who dies without Christ is covered in sin, and God cannot be reconciled to them.

This idea is widely held by Christians today and is almost always used to reinforce the doctrine of Eternal Suffering, as if this is an established fact according to the scriptures.

But, is it?

The only place we see any scriptures that suggest that God's Holiness prevents Him from being in the presence of sin is found in Habbukuk.

"Your eyes are too pure to look on evil; you cannot tolerate wrongdoing." (Habbukuk 1:13a)

But if we keep reading that chapter we might notice that Habbukuk wraps up that statement by noting that God seems to look upon the sinful anyway:

"...why do you idly look at traitors and remain silent when the wicked swallows up the man more righteous than he?" (v. 13b)

In other words, the verse begins with an assumption—*God is too holy to look upon evil*—but then the statement itself is cast into doubt as the prophet observes that God *does indeed* look on evil after all and asks: "*Why does a holy God tolerate sinners and remain silent?*"

Another verse that is often used to support this idea that God is too holy to look upon our sins is found in Isaiah where we read:

"But your iniquities have separated you from your God; your sins have hidden his face from you, so that he will not hear." (Isaiah 59:2)

But if we keep reading a bit further we see this:

"The Lord looked and was displeased that there was no justice. He saw that there was no one, he was appalled that there was no one to intervene; so his own arm achieved salvation for him, and his own righteousness sustained him." (v. 16)

"As for me, this is my covenant with them," says the Lord. "My Spirit,who is on you, will not depart from you…" (v. 21)

So, here, in the very same chapter, we read that God *does* look, and that He *does* see our sins, and that "[His] Spirit…*will not depart…*"

Finally, let's look at Jesus who was the "exact representation of the Father" (Hebrews 1:3) and "the only one who had ever seen God" and who "came to reveal the Father to us." (John 1:18)

IS JESUS TOO HOLY TO LOOK UPON SIN OR TO BE IN THE PRESENCE OF SINNERS? HARDLY! INSTEAD, THOSE SINNERS ARE HIS CLOSEST FRIENDS.

What do we notice about Jesus? Does He, as God in the flesh, avert his gaze when surrounded by sinners? Is Jesus too holy to look upon sin or to be in the presence of sinners? Hardly! Instead, those sinners are his closest friends. He spends so much time with them that the religious elite—who, by the way, *were*

too holy to spend time with sinners—openly criticized him for
it.

> "The Son of Man has come eating and drinking, and you say,
> 'Look at him! A glutton and a drunkard, a friend of tax collec-
> tors and sinners!'" (Luke 7:34)

So, is God really "too holy to look on our sin"? Absolutely
not! In fact, if God was too holy to look upon our sins, then God
would never be able to look at anyone or see anything. Instead,
we see time and again that God's eyes are always upon us,[3] and
that we cannot go anywhere to escape God's presence, even if we
were to descend into the depths of hell (Sheol) itself:

> "Where shall I go from thy spirit? Or where shall I flee from thy
> presence? If I ascend up into heaven, you are there: if I make my
> bed in hell, behold, thou art there." (Psalm 139:7-8)

*But, didn't God (the Father) turn His face away from Jesus when
he was on the cross? Wasn't that because at that moment Jesus was
taking on all the sins of the world and God could not look upon this
sin?*

On the cross, Jesus cried out, *"My God, my God! Why have
you forsaken me?"*

From this single sentence, many bible teachers and pastors
have theorized that it was in this moment that the Father looked
away from Jesus—because of all of our sins being laid upon
Jesus—and it was in this moment that Jesus experienced separation from the Father for the only time in all of eternity.

As dramatic and poetically compelling that might be, the
truth is simply this: The Bible nowhere supports this theory.

So, where does it come from?

This statement from Jesus was a quote from Psalm 22 which
begins:

> "My God, my God, why have you forsaken me? Why are you
> so far from saving me, so far from my cries of anguish?" (v. 1)

But, this is a Messianic Psalm. In this Psalm we also read prophetic statements like:

"…they pierce my hands and my feet." (v. 16)

"…They divide my clothes among them and cast lots for my garment." (v. 18)

Perhaps Jesus is quoting this Psalm because he hopes to point out how these exact words are being fulfilled in their midst?

Note especially what this same Psalm has to say about whether or not God turns away from him while this is taking place:

"For he [God] has not despised or scorned the suffering of the afflicted one; *he [God] has not hidden his face from him but has listened to his cry for help.*" (v. 24) [emphasis mine]

The Psalmist tells us that God "will *not* hide His face from him."

So, did the Father turn His face away from Jesus when He was on the cross?

No. Not even for a minute.

In fact, quite the opposite is true. Jesus affirms that His Father will never abandon Him:

"Jesus replied. "A time is coming and in fact has come when you will be scattered, each to your own home. You will leave me all alone. *Yet I am not alone, for my Father is with me.* I have told you these things so that in me you may have peace. In this world you will have trouble. But take heart! I have overcome the world." (John 16:31-33) [emphasis mine]

Jesus not only informs us that His Father will not leave him (even though the disciples will), but that this abandonment by the disciples and the faithful presence of the Father occurs at the same time: While Jesus is hanging on the cross!

This really should not surprise us. God promises all through the scriptures that He will never leave us or forsake us. Jesus even reminds us that He will be with us always, even unto the end of the age.[4]

So, to recap:

The Father did *not* look away from Jesus while He was on the cross.

God is *not* too holy to look at sin.

God will *not* leave or forsake us.

Let's examine another assumption of this view.

Every human soul is eternal. Therefore, everyone will spend eternity in either Heaven or in Hell.

This is another assertion that is often made by those who hold to the doctrine of Eternal Suffering. In their preaching, they will often say something like: "Everyone is immortal. The only question is where you will spend eternity."

But, does the Bible teach that every human soul is actually eternal? Is it really only a question of where your soul will spend eternity—in heaven or in an eternal lake of fire?

The answer overlaps a little with our examination of the doctrine of Annihilation, or Conditional Immortality. So, I will save this answer for our next chapter when we dig a bit deeper into this perspective.

For now, you should know that there are no verses in the Bible that specifically claim that every human soul is by nature eternal. Quite the opposite, actually, but we'll unpack this concept in more detail soon.

So, as we wrap up our assessment of the doctrine of Eternal Suffering, let us also note that there were approximately 14 sermons preached in the book of Acts by the Apostles.[5] Not a single one of those evangelistic messages contained any threat of eternal torment in a lake of fire.

Not one.

If Jesus affirmed this message of eternal suffering, and if the Apostles believed it, then why did no one ever teach it? How could they preach the Gospel without once mentioning it?

Allow me to suggest that perhaps the reason we don't see them preaching this is because they simply did not ever believe it.

Also, if you think a loving God would burn His children for eternity, consider that in the book of Jeremiah God stressed—three separate times—that it would never enter His mind to do such a thing:

"They have built the high places of Topheth in the Valley of Ben Hinnom to burn their sons and daughters in the fire—something I did not command, nor did it enter my mind." (Jeremiah 7:31)

"They have built the high places of Baal to burn their children in the fire as offerings to Baal—something I did not command or mention, nor did it enter my mind." (Jeremiah 19:5)

"They built high places for Baal in the Valley of Ben Hinnom to sacrifice their sons and daughters to Molek, though I never commanded—nor did it enter my mind—that they should do such a detestable thing" (Jeremiah 32:35)

Notice that two of these three verses here reference the literal Valley of Hinnom, or Gehenna. Notice that God talks about how the Israelites burned their children in Gehenna—or Hell—to appease their god. Now, notice that God says this about burning children in Gehenna to appease a divine being: *"It never entered my mind."*

That sounds like a God who loves his children more than we love our own and who would never—ever—consider burning them in Gehenna—or anywhere else—for any reason.

That's great news, isn't it?

CHAPTER 6

ANNIHILATIONISM EXAMINED

"In the end and consummation of the Universe all are to be restored into their original harmonious state, and we all shall be made one body and be united once more into a perfect man and the prayer of our Savior shall be fulfilled that all may be one."

—JEROME (347 TO 420 A.D.)

The other minority view of the afterlife held by the Christian Church from the earliest days is Conditional Immortality, or Annihilationism.

Before we dig into this one, we probably need to establish some ground rules for how we proceed. Rather than just look at the verses that appear to support this particular view, we also need to consider whether or not these verses refute the doctrine of Eternal Suffering. So, there's a lot we need to cover and more than one question we need to answer as we go along.

One big assumption that this view challenges is the one that we identified under the eternal suffering discussion: *Is every human soul eternal by nature?*

What does the Bible suggest?

1 JOHN 5:12

"Whoever has the Son has life; *whoever does not have the Son of God does not have life.*" [emphasis mine]

This is one of the strongest verses in favor of annihilationism, I believe. Here we learn that only those who are in Christ have life and that those who are not in Christ do not have life. Pretty straightforward.

What this doesn't tell us, however, is whether or not God may decide to keep human souls alive after death in order to purify and refine them by fire and bring them eventually to repentance—as we are taught in the Universalist view.

In other words, whereas the life spoken of here is guaranteed for those who have Christ now, it is also implied that those without Christ may receive life if they were to eventually embrace Christ in the future.

In fact, what the verse literally tells us is that those who have Christ—right now—have life right now. Those who do not have Christ in this life do not have the life that Christ offers to them—yet.

However, if one day those who currently do not have Christ were to eventually embrace him, then they would have life. And there's nothing here to suggest that this receiving of Christ cannot take place after death.

What's also not entirely clear in this verse is whether this has 70 AD in view. If it's meant to reference the coming destruction of Jerusalem, then the "life" that those in Christ have could merely be a reference to how they will escape the death associated with that destruction.

Another possible consideration in this case is the question of whether everyone is already "in Christ" and in what ways some are "in Christ" compared to whether Christ is in everyone or only in the faithful.

That's something we'll unpack a bit later, I promise. For now, let's look at another verse that supports the doctrine of Conditional Immortality.

1 TIMOTHY 6:15-16

"...*God*, the blessed and only Ruler, the King of kings and Lord of lords, *who alone is immortal* and who lives in unapproachable light, whom no one has seen or can see." [emphasis mine]

This would be the second most convincing verse in favor of conditional immortality since it clearly says that God alone is immortal, and therefore humans are, by definition, not immortal.

But, again, this verse speaks to the immortal nature of God. It does not rule out the possibility that humans could receive immortality as a gift from God at another time.

In fact, we do know from other verses that God does impart eternal life (or immortality) to those who are in Christ. Our previous verse is one example.

The remaining texts in favor of annihilationism speak more about the destruction of the wicked. Let's look at some of the stronger ones here:

MATTHEW 10:28

"Do not be afraid of those who kill the body but cannot kill the soul. Rather, be afraid of the one who can destroy both soul and body in hell [Gehenna]."[1]

This passage is still very much about Gehenna and therefore falls under the heading of apocalyptic hyperbole, not about what happens to us after we die.

Still, the terms used here suggest that "both body and soul" can be destroyed in this place, not tortured there forever and ever. So, even if this were a verse about the afterlife, what it tells us about is destruction, not conscious suffering.

But, if this is not about the postmortem condition of sinners, then what is the purpose of mentioning the destruction of the soul and the body?

Well, first of all, Jesus says that we should fear "the one who *can* destroy both soul and body..." but wants to point out that this does not mean that both soul and body *will be* destroyed in Gehenna. The potential for destruction is what is suggested, but it is not necessarily guaranteed or automatic.

We should also point out that there is an assumption made by most New Testament translators that Jesus is referring to God in this passage when he speaks of "the one who can destroy both soul and body." Some English translations even capitalize the word "One" here to signify that this is who Jesus is speaking about. But that is not necessarily what Jesus means to suggest here.

If we notice that Jesus rather unexpectedly uses the phrase "soul and body" rather than the more natural order of "body and soul" it may be because he is quoting from Isaiah 10:18, which also uses that same odd phrasing to say:

"The glory of his forest and of his fruitful land
the Lord will destroy, both soul and body,
and it will be as when a sick man wastes away."

In context, this verse in Isaiah is about God's judgment on the nation of Israel, which is compared to a wildfire that burns down a forest. If this is what Jesus is doing here, then he is referencing a national judgment against Israel that would mirror the one in 70 AD, which would also make sense given that Jesus mentions Gehenna.

Therefore, it's very likely that this verse—whatever it means—is not about a postmortem judgment but about a national judgment carried out by armies.

But, this still doesn't explain why Jesus would speak as if this destruction of soul and body in Gehenna would be any worse than simply having one's body destroyed.

Here's how one Bible scholar explains it:

"To the Jewish hearer, having one's corpse cast into the Valley of Hinnom [Gehenna], rather than honorably buried, would suggest a dishonorable death under the judgment and displeasure of God. This would be a matter of greater concern in a shame/honor-based culture, like that of ancient Israel, than it would be among us.

"Jesus exhortations about not fearing those who can only kill the body is given in the context of their [the disciples] facing persecution and martyrdom at the hands of ungodly men. Those dying in this way are assumed to be dying honorably for their faithfulness to God. By contrast, being cast into Gehenna suggests a disgraceful death suffered under God's judgment."[2]

1 COR. 3:17

"If anyone destroys God's temple, God will destroy that person; for God's temple is sacred, and you together are that temple."

Keep in mind that the destruction of God's temple (the Church) being described here is not an eternal destruction but a temporal one. Specifically, it is about the death of the members of the Body of Christ through persecution. So, whatever destruction is suffered by those who destroy the church may also be a

KEEP IN MIND THAT THE DESTRUCTION OF GOD'S TEMPLE (THE CHURCH) BEING DESCRIBED HERE IS NOT AN ETERNAL DESTRUCTION BUT A TEMPORAL ONE.

temporal one—in this life—and not about destruction in the afterlife.

However, if this verse was about a postmortem destruction, then we should note that it does not speak of an eternal conscious torture but about the extinction of the person.

Here are a few more verses that support conditional immortality:

Phil. 1:28

"…without being frightened in any way by those who oppose you. This is a sign to them that they will be destroyed, but that you will be saved—and that by God"

Phil. 3:19

"Their destiny is destruction, their god is their stomach, and their glory is in their shame. Their mind is set on earthly things."

As with previous verses, the destruction suffered by those who persecute the church is merely temporal and not necessarily a destruction that persists unto the afterlife.

2 Peter 2:1-3

"But there were also false prophets among the people, just as there will be false teachers among you. They will secretly introduce destructive heresies, even denying the sovereign Lord who bought them—*bringing swift destruction on themselves*. Many will follow their depraved conduct and will bring the way of truth into disrepute. In their greed these teachers will exploit you with fabricated stories. Their condemnation has long been hanging over them, and *their destruction has not been sleeping*." [emphasis mine]

2 Peter 3:7

"By the same word the present heavens and earth are reserved for fire, being kept for the day of judgment and *destruction of the ungodly.*" [emphasis mine]

In both of these verses, the destruction in view is the prophesied national judgment coming against Jerusalem and those who rejected Christ, which was fulfilled in 70 AD.

The destruction or death that is spoken of here need not necessarily refer to destruction in the afterlife and, in fact, reads most naturally as a threat of destruction, or death, in this life. Both of these verses had their fulfillment when Jerusalem was destroyed by the Romans in 70 AD.

John 3:16

"For God so loved the world that he gave his one and only Son, that whoever believes in him *shall not perish but have eternal life.*" [emphasis mine]

The perishing spoken of here is in line with what we read Jesus referring to all the time in the Gospels: *"Repent or likewise perish."* There is a final judgment coming, and the only escape is to follow the words of Christ to avoid the coming destruction, which came in 70 AD.

Even if this verse is intended to speak of what happens in the afterlife, the terms here are about perishing, not endless torture.

Romans 2:12

"All who sin apart from the law will also perish apart from the law, and all who sin under the law will be judged by the law."

Once more, a verse that speaks of death, not eternal torment. If this is about what happens after we die in this life, then it does not rule out the possibility of hope after we die.

But one way to read this passage is simply to agree at face value that people who sin apart from the law will also die apart from the law. It wouldn't be inconsistent to say that those who sin apart from the law also ride the bus apart from the law, or brush their teeth apart from the law, etc.

In other words, the statement is simply that whatever you do apart from the law, you will remain consistently apart from the law.

Romans 6:23

> "For the wages of sin is death, but the gift of God is eternal life in Christ Jesus our Lord."

What this verse does is to help us see that the wages of sin is death, not endless conscious torture.

But, does it teach that God will destroy people who die in their sins? Not necessarily. I believe the wider context of the entire chapter is that sin offers its own reward, which is death. This is in direct contrast to what God has gone out of His way to extend to everyone—eternal life in Christ—offered as a free gift that we need not earn but simply receive with thanksgiving. The clue is in the verse that comes just before this one:

> "But now that you have been set free from sin and have become slaves of God, the benefit you reap leads to holiness, and the result is eternal life." (v. 22)

The point is that *now* we have been set free from sin. Our new condition is that we belong to God, and we reap a benefit that leads to holiness—eternal life!

The overall emphasis in these two verses is eternal life, not death.

1 Thessalonians 5:2-3

> "…for you know very well that the Day of the Lord will come like a thief in the night. While people are saying, "Peace and

safety," destruction will come on them suddenly, as labor pains
on a pregnant woman, and they will not escape."

Our clue here is the phrase "Day of the Lord" in the beginning of this section. We know that this was fulfilled in 70 AD.
Therefore, this destruction is temporal, and was about physical
death, not spiritual death in the afterlife.

2 Thessalonians 1:9

"...they will be punished with everlasting destruction and shut
out from the presence of the Lord and from the glory of his
might."

2 Thessalonians 2:8

"And then the lawless one will be revealed, whom the Lord Jesus
will overthrow with the breath of his mouth and destroy by the
splendor of his coming."

Again, more apocalyptic hyperbole speaking of the lawless
one, and the "splendor of his [Christ's] coming," which we know
was in terms of national judgment, taking the form of an invading army that destroyed the city and the temple and brought
about the "end of the Jewish age."

If the destruction here is intended to be in reference to the
postmortem condition of the unrighteous, the language used
here refers to destruction, not to endless torture in a lake of fire.

SUMMARY

What we see when we look at the verses that are used to support
annihilationism, or conditional immortality, is similar to what
we see when we look at the verses used to support eternal suffering: most are not about what happens to us after we die, but

are instead about the prophesied destruction of Jerusalem which was fulfilled in 70 AD.

Even in cases where the language may or may not be a reference to that national judgment against Israel, the terms are all about death, perishing and destruction. Nothing is explicitly described concerning eternal souls being tortured forever with no hope of escape.

For those who are convinced by the Annihilationist view, I can at least understand why. There are numerous verses which speak of death and destruction. So, of the two views we've examined so far, this view has the stronger case scripturally, if you take these verses at face value.

Between the doctrines of Eternal Suffering and Conditional Immortality, at least the Conditional Immortality view does not require us to accept a God who would roast his own children for eternity.

Of these two, I would prefer the doctrine of Conditional Immortality. But we still need to look at the doctrine of Universal Reconciliation.

Keep in mind, this was the dominant view of the majority of Christians for the first 500 years. Why did they embrace this view? Where did they learn of it? Why were they not convinced by these other verses of scripture that we've already examined?

All of this and a bit more will be examined in our next chapters.

CHAPTER 7

UNIVERSAL RECONCILIATION EXAMINED

"For it is evident that God will in truth be all in all when there shall be no evil in existence, when every created being is at harmony with itself and every tongue shall confess that Jesus Christ is Lord; when every creature shall have been made one body."

—GREGORY OF NYSSA, (335 TO 390 A.D.)

The doctrine of Universal Reconciliation (or Patristic Universalism) is very misunderstood by most Christians today. However, the irony is that at one time in Church history it was the view that the vast majority of Christians embraced without question.

In fact, when Augustine wrote about his Infernalist (Eternal Torment) view of the afterlife, he freely admitted that the majority of Christians in his day believed in universalism:

> "It is quite in vain, then, that some–indeed very many–yield to merely human feelings and deplore the notion of the eternal punishment of the damned and their interminable and perpetual misery. They do not believe that such things will be. Not that they would go counter to divine Scripture—but, yielding to their own human feelings, they soften what seems harsh and give a milder emphasis to statements they believe are meant

more to terrify than to express literal truth." (Augustine, *Enchiridion*, sec. 112.)

And by "very many", Augustine meant, "the vast majority."

Notice, also, that Augustine graciously conceded in his statement that those who believed Universalism did so without going "counter to divine Scriptures" (even though they came to different conclusions than he did).

If only Christians today were as gracious to those who saw things differently.

Since there are so many misconceptions about this view, let's take some time to explain what the view teaches and to clarify what it does *not* teach.

The Universal Reconciliation view of the early Christian church contends that those who die without Christ will pass through the fire. (And as we've noted previously, this is something that all three views of the afterlife have in common.)

IN THE UNIVERSALIST VIEW, THIS FIRE OF JUDGEMENT IS DESIGNED NOT MERELY TO PUNISH, BUT TO PURIFY, CLEANSE, REFINE, AND RESTORE EVERYONE INTO RIGHT RELATIONSHIP WITH GOD.

In the Universalist view, this fire of judgement is designed not merely to punish, but to purify, cleanse, refine, and restore everyone into right relationship with God. The view also teaches that everyone will pass through this same fire—both righteous and unrighteous—and says that, eventually, everyone will be redeemed and restored to a right relationship with God.

So, this is not an "Olly Olly Oxen Free" doctrine where everyone just wakes up in a blissful heaven of endless delights after they die. Not at all. Under this doctrine, there is a judgment for everyone, and the nature of that judgment is to burn away everything in us that is not of God; to cleanse of all unrighteousness and renew a right spirit within us all.

What Biblical texts support this view?

One thing you're going to notice, as we get into this section, is just how much of the Patristic Universalist view hinges on specific statements made by the Apostle Paul. I've often said that, without Paul's writings, there would be no doctrine of Universal Reconciliation. (Some people really hate when I say that.)

Anyway, let's take a look at a few verses used to support this view:

1 TIMOTHY 4:10

> "For to this end we toil and strive, because we have our hope set on *the living God, who is the Savior of all people, especially of those who believe.*" [emphasis mine]

It's difficult to imagine what Paul could be referring to here other than what it specifically stated: "God is the savior of all people…but *especially* of those who believe."

We have two startling statements in a row to process here:

• First, that God is the savior of *all people.*

• Second, that God is *especially* the savior of those who believe.

If Paul did not intend to communicate the idea that *everyone* will eventually be saved by God, then it's difficult to imagine what he *did* intend to communicate.

Not to get too technical here, but the word in the Greek used here for "all" is the same word used in these other verses:

> "For verily I say unto you, till heaven and earth pass, not one jot or one tittle shall in any wise pass from the law, till *all* be fulfilled." (Matt. 5:18) [emphasis mine]

"But seek ye first the kingdom of God, and his righteousness; and *all* these things will be added to you as well." (Matt. 6:33) [emphasis mine]

"For everyone [*all*] who asks receives and he that seeks finds, and to him that knocks it shall be opened." (Matt. 7:8)

According to Strong's Exhaustive Concordance, this word "all—or *"pas"* [in the Greek]—means:

"including all the forms of declension; apparently a primary word; all, any, every, the whole: all, always, any, daily, ever, everyone, as many as, whosoever, etc."

In other words: All means all.

1 CORINTHIANS 15:21-22

"For as by a man came death, by a man has come also the resurrection of the dead. For as in Adam all die, so also in Christ shall all be made alive."

This appears to be a logic statement: "If X, then Y", and if so, then it would mean that "If in Adam all died, then also in Christ shall all be made alive."

We don't need to go over the meaning and use of the word "all" used here, but it is the same word used previously. And it does appear to suggest that the same form of "all" that is spoken of in terms of those who inherited the sin of Adam—and that would be everyone—is also the same "all" that are made alive through Christ.

As we've mentioned earlier, there may need to be some discussion about whether or not everyone is already "in Christ," or if there could be a case made that only some are "in Christ" and others are not. We will explore that very soon.

For now, let's continue to look at other verses used to support universalism:

EPHESIANS 1:7-10

"In him [Christ] we have redemption through his blood, the forgiveness of our trespasses, according to the riches of his grace, which he lavished upon us, in all wisdom and insight making known to us the mystery of *his will,* according to *his purpose,* which he set forth *in Christ as a plan for the fullness of time, to unite all things in him,* things in heaven and things on earth." [emphasis mine]

Once more, Paul employs the use of the word "all" to denote the salvation of everyone through Christ in "the fullness of time."

God's purpose, Paul says, is tied to the "mystery of his will" and is "set forth in Christ...to unite all things in him...," and those "all things" must of necessity include "all people" whether in heaven or on the earth.

ROMANS 5:18-19

"Therefore, as one trespass led to condemnation for all men, *so one act of righteousness leads to justification and life for all men.* For as by the one man's disobedience the many were made sinners, so by the one man's obedience *the many will be made righteous.*" [emphasis mine]

This is quite similar to the first verse we examined (1 Cor. 15:21-22) where Paul compares and contrasts the work and ministry of Adam with the work and ministry of Jesus. In doing so, Paul leaves us very little wiggle room to read this any other way than what it plainly appears to say: *That in the same way everyone was made a sinner due to Adam's sin, everyone will be made righteous because of Christ's obedience.*

PAUL LEAVES US VERY LITTLE WIGGLE ROOM TO READ THIS ANY OTHER WAY THAN WHAT IT PLAINLY APPEARS TO SAY: THAT IN THE SAME WAY EVERYONE WAS MADE A SINNER DUE TO ADAM'S SIN, EVERYONE WILL BE MADE RIGHTEOUS BECAUSE OF CHRIST'S OBEDIENCE.

What else could he mean? To suggest that the "many" who were made sinners by Adam's disobedience doesn't mean "everyone" is to say that not everyone was born a sinner. But, of course, that can't be what Paul means here.

However, if we try to say that the "many" who "will be made righteous" is less than "everyone"—which may be easy to do—then we have to affirm that the "many" made sinners by Adam's disobedience are also not "everyone."

Paul has really put us in a pickle here. We can't have it both ways.

I think we can choose one or the other option, but we cannot mix and match these conditions. To do so is to break the entire train of thought that Paul intends to use to make his point.

We may disagree on the point that Paul is making, but I don't believe we can avoid choosing at least one of the two possible options.

Either some were made sinners due to Adam's disobedience, and therefore only some are made righteous because of Christ's obedience, OR everyone was made a sinner due to Adam's disobedience, and therefore everyone will be made righteous by Christ's obedience.

As New Testament scholar David Bentley Hart says in his commentary regarding this verse:

"From the context, one can tell what [Paul] is saying: that just as one transgression (or the transgression of one man) brought condemnation to all human beings, so by one rectifying act (or the rectifying act of one man) all human beings receive a rectification of life (meaning either a rectification of their lives, or a rectification imparted by the life of the risen Christ)...the strict proportionality of the formulation, however, is quite clear, here and in the surrounding verses: just as the first sin brought condemnation and death to absolutely everyone, so Christ's act of righteousness brings righteousness and life to absolutely everyone. Whether intentional or not, the plain meaning of the verse is that of universal condemnation annulled by universal salvation."[1]

COLOSSIANS 1:14; 19-20

"For in him [Christ] *all* the fullness of God was pleased to dwell, and through him to reconcile to himself *all* things, whether on earth or in heaven, making peace by the blood of his cross." [emphasis mine]

At first glance, this verse appears pretty straightforwardly another example of Paul using the word "all" to teach that Christ will reconcile everyone to himself. And that is most certainly what this is. But if we look closer we'll notice that Paul—once again—uses the term "all" twice in the same verse. This time, rather than contrast the "all" who sin in Adam with the "all" who are made alive in Christ, Paul seems to compare "all" the fullness of God which dwells in Christ with the "all" who will be reconciled through him.

This is yet another difficult passage to diffuse. If we try to say that the "all" who are reconciled is somehow limited in scope, then we must also make room for "all" the fullness of God in Christ to be just as limited in scope. Yet, the passage will not allow for this. We are left to either affirm the boundless range of the meaning of "all" in both cases, or to limit the reach of this term in equal measures. Quite frankly, this cannot be done. Just as no one can limit the degree to which "all the fullness of God" dwells in Christ, no one dare limit the reconciliation of "all" who receive peace through the blood of his cross.

This is a very strong verse for universal reconciliation, indeed.

PHILIPPIANS 2:10-11

"…that at the name of Jesus every knee should bow, in heaven and on earth and under the earth, and every tongue *gladly* confess that Jesus Christ is Lord, to the glory of God the Father." [emphasis mine]

I've added the word "gladly" here for a very good reason: Most English translations mistakenly omit it. Yet, the word for "confess" used here is the Greek word *"exomologeō"* which means *"to profess openly and joyfully."*

All my life I've been told to read this verse as if those who bend their knees and confess Jesus as Lord do so only under protest; as if the words will be spit out of clenched teeth and their bowing down will be under protest. But that's not at all what this verse actually says.

Why would anyone leave out this word "gladly" unless they hoped to use this verse to teach exactly what I've just described? In other words, I believe that this word is left out of our English translations intentionally; to support the doctrine of Eternal Suffering and to obscure the clear teaching that one day everyone, everywhere will *gladly and joyfully confess* that Jesus Christ is their Lord, to the glory of God the Father.

Remember what Paul says about those who confess that Jesus Chris is their Lord?

"…That *if you confess with your mouth the Lord Jesus* and believe in your heart that God has raised Him from the dead, *you will be saved.*" (Rom. 10:9) [emphasis mine]

Perhaps this is another reason why the word "gladly" is left out of our Bibles in the Philippians passage; because it might invite such a clear conclusion as this—that, eventually, *everyone* will confess Jesus Christ as Lord, and that *everyone* will be saved.

1 CORINTHIANS 3:11-15

"For no one can lay any foundation other than the one already laid, which is Jesus Christ. If anyone builds on this foundation using gold, silver, costly stones, wood, hay or straw, their work will be shown for what it is, because the Day will bring it to light. It will be *revealed with fire, and the fire will test the quality of each person's work.* If what has been built survives, the builder will receive a reward. *If it is burned up, the builder will suffer loss but yet will be saved—even though only as one escaping through the flames.*" [emphasis mine]

This passage has already been alluded to a few times so far, but it's where we get the idea that everyone will pass through the fire—both the righteous and the unrighteous—and also where we see that the purpose of the fire is to reveal and refine, not torture and destroy.

We also see that even those whose works are found to be worthless and burned away will still be saved—"even though only as one escaping through the flames."

So, rather than affirming the notion that only those who are righteous will be saved, this verse suggests that both the righteous and the unrighteous alike will pass through the fire and be saved, regardless of whether their lives are shown to produce "gold, silver and costly stones" or "wood, hay and stubble."

What an astounding verse about universal reconciliation.

HEBREWS 12:6-11

"My son, *do not despise the chastening of the Lord,*
Nor be discouraged when you are rebuked by Him;
For whom the Lord loves He chastens,
And scourges every son whom He receives."

"*If you endure chastening, God deals with you as with sons; for*
what son is there whom a father does not chasten? But if you are
without chastening, of which *all have become partakers*, then
you are illegitimate and not sons. Furthermore, we have had
human fathers who corrected us, and we paid them respect.
Shall we not much more readily be in subjection to the Father of
spirits and live? For they indeed for a few days chastened us as
seemed best to them, *but He for our profit, that we may be par-*
takers of His holiness. Now no chastening seems to be joyful for
the present, but painful; nevertheless, afterward it yields the peace-
able fruit of righteousness to those who have been trained by it."
[emphasis mine]

This passage in Hebrews is a very foundational verse for the
doctrine of Universal Reconciliation, because it includes several key ideas that speak to the nature and purpose of God's
correction.

First: God chastens (or disciplines) those He loves.

If we believe what Jesus says in John 3:16, then we know
that God loves the whole world. Therefore, God will chasten everyone. This is an expression of God's love for us, not His wrath.

In fact, the verse affirms that we *all have become partakers* of God's
discipline.

Secondly, because we understand that our earthly fathers disciplined

> **IF WE BELIEVE WHAT JESUS SAYS IN JOHN 3:16, THEN WE KNOW THAT GOD LOVES THE WHOLE WORLD. THEREFORE, GOD WILL CHASTEN EVERYONE. THIS IS AN EXPRESSION OF GOD'S LOVE FOR US, NOT HIS WRATH.**

us, we should submit to our Heavenly Father's discipline "and live." (v. 9)

The promise here is that after we endure our Heavenly Father's discipline, the result is that we will live, or receive life. (Not that we will be disciplined and die or suffer endlessly.)

Next, God disciplines us "for our profit, that we may be partakers of His holiness."

This is huge. God's reason for disciplining us is not only because He loves us, and not only so that we may live, but this discipline is "for our profit." In other words, it's done with our benefit in mind, and this specifically is so that "we may be partakers of His holiness."

Boom.

Notice here that there is no fork in the road. Everyone endures discipline. Everyone is treated as a son or daughter. Everyone becomes a partaker of His holiness.

> GOD'S REASON FOR DISCIPLINING US IS NOT ONLY BECAUSE HE LOVES US, AND NOT ONLY SO THAT WE MAY LIVE, BUT THIS DISCIPLINE IS "FOR OUR PROFIT." IN OTHER WORDS, IT'S DONE WITH OUR BENEFIT IN MIND, AND THIS SPECIFICALLY IS SO THAT "WE MAY BE PARTAKERS OF HIS HOLINESS."

Finally, we see that this discipline is "painful", yet it has one end result: "the peaceable fruit of righteousness for those who have been trained by it."

Righteousness, holiness, profit, and life are the words used here to describe the discipline we all receive from God, our Father. This is because He loves us. It's not about wrath. It's not about torture. It's not about beating us for all eternity because we were born into a world of sin.

God, we see, is a loving father—and a much better father than any of us could ever be. He loves us. He disciplines us for our profit. He responds to our sins by forgiving us. He does not beat the disease of sin out of us. He heals us and restores us and makes us partakers of His holiness forever.

Of course, this particular verse is especially conditional to the question of whether or not everyone is a child of God, or if only Christians are truly considered the children of God.

In addition, we should also explore the question we've been alluding to for a few chapters now: *Are all in Christ, or is Christ only in those who call themselves "Christians"?*

That's what we'll look at next.

CHAPTER 8

WHO IS IN CHRIST?

"We can set no limits to the agency of the Redeemer to redeem, to rescue, to discipline in his work, and so will he continue to operate after this life."

—CLEMENT OF ALEXANDRIA, (150 TO 215 A.D.)

The doctrine of Universal Reconciliation teaches that God wants everyone to be saved and wills that none should perish. Since God alone has the power to redeem and restore everyone to Himself, God has exerted this power through Christ who came to reconcile the world to Himself.

The punishment endured in the afterlife is intended to correct and restore everyone into a right relationship with God. This is how God treats His children (as we have just seen in Hebrews 12:10).

But, is *everyone* a child of God? Or are Christians the only legitimate children of God?

Some suggest that it is only those who are "in Christ" who are rightly

SOME SUGGEST THAT IT IS ONLY THOSE WHO ARE "IN CHRIST" WHO ARE RIGHTLY CALLED GOD'S CHILDREN. BUT, THEN WE HAVE TO ASK, "ISN'T EVERYONE ALREADY IN CHRIST?"

called God's children. But, then we have to ask, "Isn't everyone already in Christ?"

These are difficult questions to answer, as we'll soon see. But we may be able to at least shed some light on the issue and work out the answers together.

WHO ARE THE CHILDREN OF GOD?

Well, as with many Christian doctrines, the Bible is not perfectly clear on this point. At least, not at first glance.

For example, there are several verses that affirm the notion that God is the Father of all humanity. As when the Apostle Paul spoke to the idol-worshipping pagans in Athens and confirmed that:

> "Indeed, *[God] is actually not far from each one of us,* for in him we live and move and exist; as also some of your own poets have put it, *"For we are his offspring."'* (Acts 17:26-28) [emphasis mine]

And as Paul also said to the Ephesians:

> "For this reason I bow my knees to *the Father of our Lord Jesus Christ,* from whom *the whole family in heaven and earth is named…"* (Eph. 3:14-15) [emphasis mine]

We also have an example in the Gospels where, as author Brad Jersak points out:

> "…in Luke's version of the genealogy of Jesus Christ, he begins with our Lord, then works his way back: "son of… son of… son of…" all the way to "the son of Adam, the son of God" (Luke 3:38). We are *all* God's children by virtue of creation. As Creator, God is our Father and we are *all* his children."[1]

If these were our only verses on the question, we could stop right here. However, the Bible is not univocal on the topic, and so we have to consider these other verses which suggest that

being the child of God is something conferred upon the faithful
followers of Christ alone. For example:

> "Yet to all who did receive him (Christ), *to those who believed in
> his name, he gave the right to become children of God.*" (John
> 1:12) [emphasis mine]

This seems pretty straightforward. If you trust in Christ then
you are the child of God. If not, then you are not a child of God.
What could be more clear?

Well, not so fast. What's being said here is a bit more nuanced
than the English translation may suggest. The phrase "*those who
believed in his name*" is more properly wrought as "*those who put
their full trust in Him*". In other words, the ones who put the
teachings of Christ into practice daily are those who are more
properly considered to have "*the right to become the children of
God.*"

Why does that distinction matter? Because several times Jesus
refers to this idea of imitation as an indication of how we reveal
who our Father is.

> "But I say to you, *love your enemies* and pray for those who
> persecute you, *so that you may be sons of your Father who is in
> heaven;* for He causes His sun to rise on the evil and the good,
> and sends rain on the righteous and the unrighteous." (Matt.
> 5:44-45) [emphasis mine]

Jesus also gives us a negative example of how our behavior might reveal whose children we are when he confronts the
Pharisees:

> "*I know that you are Abraham's descendants,* but you seek to kill
> Me, because My word has no place in you. *I speak what I have
> seen with My Father, and you do what you have seen with your
> father.*"

> "They answered and said to Him, "*Abraham is our father.*"

"Jesus said to them, "*If you were Abraham's children, you would do the works of Abraham*. But now you seek to kill Me, a Man who has told you the truth which I heard from God. Abraham did not do this. *You do the deeds of your father.*"

"… Jesus said to them, "*If God were your Father, you would love Me*, for I proceeded forth and came from God; nor have I come of Myself, but He sent Me. Why do you not understand My speech? Because you are not able to listen to My word. *You are of your father the devil, and the desires of your father you want to do.*" (John 8:17-44) [emphasis mine]

In this case, Jesus begins by affirming that Abraham is their Father, but then suggests that their murderous hearts make it appear as if their Father is the Devil.

Again, Brad Jersak explains:

"In other words, "children of Abba" are those who act like Abba in their indiscriminate and inclusive grace. This more exclusive use of "children" is not about Christian confession, but about imitation.

"…In short, Christ's call to imitate Abba is to "Be what you are." It is to make the truth of your being (children of God) the way of your being (imitation of Abba).

"So too, in the Beatitudes, it is not the Christians but the peacemakers who "will be called the children of God" (Matt. 5:9). That's because peacemakers are reproducing Abba's work of reconciliation "on earth as it is in heaven."

"Is Christ denying that everyone is a child of God? No. Is Christ denying that Christians are children of God? No. That's just not how he's using "sons" in these verses. He's saying something about how children are recognized as they imitate their parents."[2]

So, in one sense, everyone alive is a child of God who can rightly call God their "Father," but, in another sense, it is only those who are living out of the reality of their intimate connection with God who can rightly call God "Abba" or "Father."

All humanity is created in the image of God and we are all one family. Some are more aware of this reality than others. Those who reflect the character and nature of their Heavenly Father are "children of God" in a deeper sense, but not in any exclusive sense. As we read here:

> "So we have come to know and to believe the love that God has for us. *God is love, and whoever abides in love abides in God, and God abides in him.*" (1 John 4:16) [emphasis mine]

The overall testimony of scripture is that God is the Father of all humanity. God's love for everyone is expressed in the sending of Christ who told us that God is like the prodigal son's father who never stopped loving his child, even when he lived a life of rebellion and tried to run as far away from him as possible.

God never disowns us. God never stops being our Father. We never stop being children of God. Even on our worst day, God's love for us is based on who God is, not on who we are, or what we do.

Yes, we can reflect our sonship or daughterhood more clearly whenever we love others, serve others or forgive others. But, even if we fail to do this, it doesn't change the fact that God is our Father, and that we are loved and forgiven. Based on our behavior, it may appear that our father is the devil, at times. But this is not the reality. It is a perversion of the reality. God is our Father, and we are all His children. If we reflect the character of Christ, then we are starting to look like our Father more and more. This is the way it's supposed to work.

> GOD NEVER DISOWNS US. GOD NEVER STOPS BEING OUR FATHER. WE NEVER STOP BEING CHILDREN OF GOD. EVEN ON OUR WORST DAY, GOD'S LOVE FOR US IS BASED ON WHO GOD IS, NOT ON WHO WE ARE, OR WHAT WE DO.

IS EVERYONE ALREADY IN CHRIST?

The answer to this question is very similar to the previous question, in that the scriptures are not totally clear on this point. We have to look at a range of passages and determine the nuances between the various examples given.

Let's start with the question of whether we are all in God before we move to the question of whether we are all in Christ. (And then we'll look at whether Christ is in all of us, or only in some of us).

Are we all in God?

There's an old joke that goes like this: *One fish says to another fish, "How's the water?" and the other fish says, "What is water?"*

The point is that, to the fish, "water" isn't a thing. It's just the world it was born into. So, it doesn't know what being wet is, or understand the difference between air and water either.

Here's another analogy: We are all in God. God is inescapable. God is our "water," and most of us have no idea that we are all surrounded by God.

This is odd, especially for Christians, since we have several verses in our Bibles that suggest exactly this; that wherever we go, God is there—even if we descend into the grave (see Psalms 139:7-16), and that God is "the one in whom we all live and move and have our being" (see Acts 17:28).

Here's what New Testament scholar David Bentley Hart has to say about this:

> "Ladies and gentleman, we are inside of God. Always. There is nowhere we can go to escape God. Whether in "heaven" or in "hell" or any location or state of consciousness we can

conceptualize. There is no "separation". Ever. No reality can exist in and of itself, or be self-sustained or void of God's presence. To find one's self within the realm of being is to find one's self in the mystery of God, the actualizer and energizer of being. For out of and through and into him are all things. All things. Which includes all things.

> "God is not only the ultimate reality that the intellect and the will seek but is also the primordial reality with which all of us are always engaged in every moment of existence and consciousness, apart from which we have no experience of anything whatsoever. Or, to borrow the language of Augustine, God is not only 'superior summon meo'—beyond my utmost heights—but also 'interior intimo meo'—more inward to me than my inmost depths."[3]

So, we are all immersed and surrounded by God. Not only this, but if God is love, then we are all—always—surrounded by perfect love.

That's good news.

This also means that if we are all in God, then there is no one who is outside of God or far from God's reach.

God is near to us. Closer than our own breath, nearer than our own heartbeat.

This is really good news.

We also have verses like this one which suggest that God is in everyone:

> "There is one body and one Spirit, just as you were called to one hope when you were called; one Lord, one faith, one baptism; *one God and Father of all, who is over all and through all and in all.*" (Eph. 4:4-6) [emphasis mine]

Not only is God "the Father of all," He is also "in all" of us. That's pretty amazing.

So, it would appear that we could make a very strong case that God is in all of us. But, what about Christ? Is Christ in all of us, or only in some of us?

Is everyone in Christ?

Now, we've already looked at Paul's sermon to those pagans in Athens where he told them that they were in Christ, *"the one in whom we all live and move and have our being."* But in what way were these unbelieving pagans "in Christ"?

Certainly they were not "in Christ" to the same degree that the followers of Jesus were. But, where do we draw the line? What's the difference?

Well, for one thing, Jesus suggests that he is "in" every needy person we serve:

> "I'm telling you the truth: when you did it to one of the least of my brothers and sisters, you did it to me." (Matt. 25:37-40)

But, this could be a way of speaking rather than an actual reality. In other words, Jesus could be saying that it is "as if" we are serving him whenever we serve the poor, the prisoner, the naked, etc. without intending to say that he *actually* inhabits every one of those people. Otherwise, would we assume that Christ is *not* inhabiting those who are not poor, or who are not in prison, or naked? Is Christ only "in" these specific people? That's probably not what Jesus intends to say here.

At the same time, it's possible that what Jesus means to communicate is that he is already within everyone, and therefore whenever we serve anyone—not only these people, but anyone—we are also serving him.

This is closer to what many of the early church believed: that in the Incarnation Christ took on more than his own humanity, but, in effect, united himself with all of humanity. This is part of what Paul communicates when he positions Christ as the "New Adam" who has come to reframe all humanity under a new reality.

> "For as by a man came death, by a man has come also the resurrection of the dead. For as in Adam all die, so also in Christ shall all be made alive." (1 Cor. 15:21-22)

So, it's at least possible that Christ is already in all of us simply because God, the Creator of the Universe, humbled himself and became one of us, and is therefore "one with us" in much deeper way than we ever thought possible.

Combine this idea with what Paul says here:

> "But when it pleased God...*to reveal His Son in me.*" (Gal. 1:15-16) [emphasis mine]

Notice he says that God was pleased to "reveal His Son *in* me" and not that God was pleased to "reveal His Son *to* me." This suggests at least the possibility that Christ was *already* in Paul, and God only needed to reveal this Christ in him.

However, as with our previous question above, there are certain scriptures which may cast some doubt on the indwelling reality of Christ in all of us.

For example, here are some verses that appear to suggest that Christ is *only* in those who are intentionally following the teachings of Jesus:

> "Here there is no Gentile or Jew, circumcised or uncircumcised, barbarian, Scythian, slave or free, *but Christ is all, and is in all.*" (Col. 3:11) [emphasis mine]

This verse says that "Christ is in all", but it does beg the question: Is it possible that Christ really *is* already in everyone? Or does Paul only mean to say that, "here in the Body of Christ" this is true for "all" of us (Christians)?

Hold that thought, because here's another verse that challenges the idea that Christ is already in everyone:

"Examine yourselves to see whether you are in the faith; test yourselves. *Do you not realize that Christ Jesus is in you—unless, of course, you fail the test?* And I trust that you will discover that we have not failed the test." (2 Cor. 13:5-6) [emphasis mine]

So, this verse seems to suggest that maybe only those who are "in the faith" have "Christ Jesus in (them)" and that we need to test ourselves to see if it's true or not.

However, another way to read this text might be to point out that Paul wants them to stop and realize that Christ Jesus *is* in them, and the idea of a test is meant to question whether they are living as if this is true or not. Much like the dialog between Jesus and the Pharisees where he affirms that they are the children of Abraham, but then goes on to say that, based on their behavior, it *appears* as if they are the children of the Devil.

Another verse to consider is this one:

"You, however, are not in the realm of the flesh but are in the realm of the Spirit, *if indeed the Spirit of God lives in you. And if anyone does not have the Spirit of Christ, they do not belong to Christ. But if Christ is in you,* though the body is dead because of sin, the spirit is life because of righteousness." (Rom. 8:9-10) [emphasis mine]

This verse also seems to suggest that there is an "if/then" scenario being discussed: *If* we are in Christ, *then* we belong to Christ. Or, *If* Christ is in you, *then* you have the spirit of life in you. But it may also be possible, according to this verse, that the Spirit of Christ does *not* live in you, and, if so, then you do not belong to Christ.

What's going on here? Well, it's not totally clear. One could make the case that, as in the previous question, there are certain ways in which Christ is in everyone, but some of us reveal this truth by how we embody this reality.

Or, it could be that we are all in Christ—the one in whom we live and move and have our being—but Christ is not necessarily IN all of us unless we intentionally abide in Him.

In other words: If we abide in Christ, then Christ abides in us. And that "abiding" is more than simply breathing, it's an intentional decision to embrace the life of Christ that is all around us, and to embody Christ in our daily life.

So, in some ways, we are all "in Christ" or "in God," but in another sense only some are intentionally "in Christ," because they have made a choice to live intentionally out of the life of Christ by abiding in Him daily.

> SO, IN SOME WAYS, WE ARE ALL "IN CHRIST" OR "IN GOD," BUT IN ANOTHER SENSE ONLY SOME ARE INTENTIONALLY "IN CHRIST," BECAUSE THEY HAVE MADE A CHOICE TO LIVE INTENTIONALLY OUT OF THE LIFE OF CHRIST BY ABIDING IN HIM DAILY.

For example, it's possible that we are "in Christ" the same way that an empty water bottle with the cap on top can be submerged deep in the center of the ocean. The bottle is in the ocean because it is surrounded by the ocean on all sides. But the ocean is not in the bottle. This is a very important distinction to make. The bottle can be in the ocean without the ocean being inside the bottle. And perhaps this analogy can help us to understand in what ways we are in Christ but Christ may not necessarily be in us.

The only way for the ocean to enter the water bottle is for someone to take the cap off and allow the ocean to flood inside of it.

So, we may be submerged in the ocean of Christ, but Christ is not inside of us until we consciously open ourselves up to Him and allow Christ to abide in us—so we can abide in Him.

As I said, there are different ways to understand the scriptures when it comes to these questions. A very strong case can be made that we are all the children of God and that God is the Father of all. We can also make a very strong case that everyone is in God because God's presence is everywhere, and we cannot escape God no matter what we do.

But, when it comes to the question of whether everyone is in Christ or if Christ is in everyone, we may have some difficulty proving things one way or the other. Some are very convinced that Christ is in everyone based on the scriptures that we've looked at. Others, like me, are still not totally convinced and see a slight distinction between being in Christ and having Christ in us. At least in the fullest sense where we intentionally live out of the life of Christ and abide with Christ daily.

Whatever your conviction, I do still believe that we can agree on some very important realities that help us to see more clearly what the character of God is like and who we are in Christ.

Personally, I do still believe that everyone will eventually chose to be in Christ, one way or the other. But either way, I think this is still a choice that must be made, whether on this side of the grave or on the other.

As David Bentley Hart points out, no rational person would ever willingly refuse absolute love, joy, peace, and acceptance which is embodied in Christ Jesus our Lord. On this side of the grave, we see through a glass darkly; we do not see God revealed to us in all of His unveiled Glory. But, one day, this veil will be removed, and we will all see God face-to-face at last.

Once all of our misconceptions about God are erased; once we can truly see God who is Love Incarnate in this fashion, no one could ever resist this pure, irresistible, perfect love for very long.

In other words, the God that people reject in this life is not truly God as God is. What people reject is God as they understand God. That is something very different.

Again, David Bentley Hart makes an excellent point in this regard when he says:

> "Even if a sinner's deeds were infinitely evil in every objective sense...still the intentionality of a finite will...could never in perfect clarity of mind match the sheer nihilistic scope of the evil it perpetrates. Nor could any rational will that has ever enjoyed full freedom...resist the love of God willfully for eternity.

> "...The more one is in one's right mind—the more, that is, that one is conscious of God as the Goodness that fulfills all beings, and the more one recognizes that one's own nature can have its true completion and joy nowhere but in him [God]...the more inevitable is one's surrender to God. Liberated from all ignorance, emancipated from all the adverse conditions of this life, the rational soul could freely will only its own union with God, and thereby its own supreme beatitude. We are, as it were, doomed to happiness, so long as our natures follow their healthiest impulses unhindered; we cannot not will the satisfaction of our beings in our true final end...

> "...[we have] a nature whose proper end has been fashioned in harmony with a supernatural purpose. God has made us for himself, as Augustine would say, and our hearts are restless till they rest in him."[4]

But, if this is the case—if all really are saved in the end—then why follow Christ? Why evangelize? What's the point if we're all going to wind up in Heaven no matter what?

That sounds like a great thing to explore in our next chapter.

CHAPTER 9

WHY FOLLOW CHRIST IF ALL ARE SAVED?

"The wicked who have committed evil the whole period of their lives shall be punished till they learn that, by continuing in sin, they only continue in misery. And when, by this means, they shall have been brought to fear God, and to regard Him with good will, they shall obtain the enjoyment of His grace."

—THEODORE OF MOPSUESTIA, (350 TO 428 A.D.)

"So, how can we make sure we go to heaven?"

The little boy stood his ground. His mother was doing her best to answer his questions, which started out with, "Who is God?" and continued on to cover things like, "How do we talk to God?" and "What is God like?"

Up until this point, her answers were less than convincing. She had not spent much time in church herself as a young girl growing up in a small town in Tennessee. Her father had been a sharecropper, and that meant that everyone had to be out in the fields working from sunup to sundown, every single day of the week. Including Sundays.

So, their family never spent hours inside a church building all dressed up pretty, as if they had money to burn on fancy clothes.

No one could afford to waste daylight when there was so much work to be done.

Now she was in her mid-twenties, married, with one young son to care for, and a lot of bills to pay.

Her son's questions had started innocently enough that afternoon, but she quickly realized her son wasn't satisfied with any of her answers.

"So, how can we make sure we go to heaven, Mom?"

He looked up at her with his innocent eyes full of expectancy. She knew that she assumed she had the answers to these questions. She was his mother, after all. Parents are expected to know everything. But, in this case, she was out of her element.

For a moment she was tempted to make up something along the lines of Santa Claus or the Tooth Fairy. But one look at her son looking up at her—his eyes full of anticipation, and his heart quivering for answers—and she knew she could never do that to him.

Instead, she got down on her knees in front of him there in the kitchen and looked into his eyes. "I don't know, honey," she said.

The little boy looked down at the floor. She could see that he was struggling with her response. When he looked back up at her, his blue eyes were hidden behind a layer of tears which started rolling down his cheeks.

"But...we have to find out, Mom. We have to find out!"

All she could do was hold him while he cried in her arms. That's when his Dad came home from work and found them there on the floor, in front of the refrigerator.

"What's wrong?" he asked.

His wife just looked up at him and shook her head. She honestly didn't know what to say. But, she knew that their son needed to know the answers to these big questions about God.

And she wondered where they would ever get the answers that would satisfy his heart, or her own.

Eventually, that family moved to a small town in Southwest Texas on the border of Mexico called "Eagle Pass." It was an even smaller town than the one they'd left behind in Tennessee. But, after nearly ending their marriage a few months earlier, this was a fresh start for them as a family.

Propelled by their son's questions about God, they started visiting various churches around town. A Methodist church seemed to fit the bill. They attended for a few months, and even joined the choir together. But after a weekend visit at the pastor's house revealed that their preacher didn't actually believe in God, they decided to move on.

For a short time, they even looked into Mormonism. But that, too, proved disappointing.

Somehow, they found this little tiny church on a hilltop called "The Lighthouse Freewill Baptist Church." The young pastor was fresh from North Carolina with his wife and two children. They had recently started this little church and were encouraged by how quickly it was growing.

One Sunday morning, the little boy heard the answers to his questions coming from the pastor's sermon. Suddenly, it all started to make sense. He needed to come forward and ask Jesus into his heart so he could know God and go to heaven. It was so simple.

But when the music started to play, the little boy's feet were frozen to the floor. Try as he might, he couldn't make them obey his commands to move.

Soon, the music stopped. The pastor led everyone in a closing prayer.

It was over. He had missed his chance. After all this time. All this searching. Just like that, he had missed his chance to finally know God and make sure he was going to heaven.

He tapped his dad on the arm and said, "Dad, can you please tell the pastor that I wanted to go up there just now, but I couldn't move?"

His father looked down at him for a moment and then said something the boy would never forget. "No, I won't," his Dad said. "But I'll go up there with you and then you can tell him yourself. Okay?"

The little boy nodded. "Okay," he said.

Then his Father took his hand and walked up to the pastor who was still greeting people at the altar. "Pastor?" his Dad said. "My son, Keith, has something he wants to tell you."

As the little boy started to talk, the tears began to flow down his cheeks uncontrollably. He was doing it! He was going to meet God now. It was all going to be all right.

After he and the pastor prayed together, the little boy felt much better. In fact, he felt like he could fly. His feet hardly touched the ground for the next few weeks until his baptism Sunday came. That's when he and his Mom and Dad, were all baptized together during the same service. His family was saved. His questions, for now, were answered.

But there would be many more questions to come as the years rolled on. Questions that would take him even further down the road from that tiny Texas church than he could ever imagine.

As you might have guessed, that little boy was—is—me. I left out the part about how the baptistry was full of giant, Texas-sized cockroaches that we had to fish out of the water before we could start the service. I also left out some of the finer details about how we almost became Mormons and how my parent's separation, and eventual divorce and reconciliation, played into everything that eventually led us to that little town on the border of Mexico. But you get the idea.

The reason I shared that story is two-fold: 1) I love remembering how I first came to know Jesus, and 2) I wanted to show you how my entry into the faith was more about a sincere curiosity about who God was and not at all about escaping an eternity in hell.

In fact, I don't think anyone ever really talked to me very much about hell until after I had come into the faith. That's when I found out that everyone I knew who wasn't a Christian like me was going to spend eternity in the lake of fire if I didn't tell them about Jesus and get them to pray the same prayer that I had prayed that Sunday morning.

Unfortunately, I was too young to realize that I couldn't talk anyone into having the same sincere curiosity about God that I had developed as a young boy. It wasn't fear that drew me to God. It was a desire to know God better that led me, and my family, to seek out the answers. If I could have taken the time to understand that, or if someone else could have explained it to me, maybe I wouldn't have spent so many years feeling so guilty for not evangelizing my friends. Maybe I wouldn't have tried and failed to convert my younger cousin, Jimmy, on my Grandmother's front porch that next summer. Maybe I wouldn't have slapped Jimmy across the face in frustration when he mocked my faith and laughed at my zeal for God.

Maybe. But, the truth is, we'll never know.

I actually did spend a lot of time telling other people that they were going to burn in hell forever for their sins. I started a Christian band in college, and we went around singing songs and preaching this threatening gospel to everyone in El Paso who would listen to us. Some even responded to our message. We felt really great about that. We believed were doing the Lord's work.

NOT ONLY WAS THE GOSPEL NOT ABOUT SAYING A PRAYER SO YOU COULD GO TO HEAVEN WHEN YOU DIE, IT WAS ALSO NOT ABOUT A GOD WHO THREATENED TO TORTURE HIS CHILDREN FOREVER AND EVER IF THEY DIDN'T LOVE HIM IN RETURN.

Eventually, I started to realize—many years too late—that this gospel that threatened people with fear wasn't really the gospel at all. Not only was the gospel not about saying a prayer so you could go to heaven when you die, it was also not about a God who threatened to torture His children forever and ever if they didn't love Him in return.

Since I've started to teach against the doctrine of eternal suffering, I've heard the question numerous times: *"If the doctrine of Eternal Torment isn't true, why preach the gospel at all?"*

Honestly, this question really disturbs me. I think it's because it makes me wonder if the Christians who ask me this question are only Christians because they don't want to burn in hell for eternity. Perhaps if eternal suffering wasn't true, they might reconsider their decision to become a Christian in the first place.

Of course, this is because we evangelize with fear. Thousands, perhaps millions, of Christians today are in the fold simply because they were told that repeating a prayer of repentance would help them escape the fires of hell. They're only here because they're afraid of that torture. So, they bowed their heads and raised their hands, or walked the aisle and got on their knees and did whatever they had to do to avoid that awful, horrific, endless torture in the lake of fire.

So, when someone like me starts to suggest that there are two other Christian doctrines about the afterlife, and neither one involves an eternity in the fires of hell, people start to get angry, and confused. They want to know, "If hell isn't forever, then why preach the gospel? What's the point?"

My response to those who ask me this question is pretty simple: If knowing Christ doesn't make your heart sing, and if your daily walk with Jesus isn't a reward enough, then I'm not sure I can explain it to you.

Without Jesus there is no life. Without Jesus there is no love, or peace, or joy.

Why evangelize others if God doesn't plan to torture people forever in the lake of fire? Because Jesus is the best thing about being alive, and there's nothing in the world more amazing than knowing Him!

This question reveals that many Christians who ask it really haven't fully experienced the beauty of being in communion with the Creator of the universe.

"If hell does not exist, then why bother being a Christian?"

I like how Brad Jersak answers the question:

"If your only reason for being a Christian is to avoid hell, I wonder if you have ever encountered the love of our precious Savior. Have you met Him? We follow Jesus because He loves us and we love Him. We give ourselves to Jesus because He is Lord, because He purchased us with His own blood, and because our Salvation is His reward as much as it is ours. If our only reason for being a Christian is to avoid hell, we may be there already."[1]

Why evangelize if hell isn't forever?

Because His love is better than life.

Because in His presence are joys everlasting.

Because He has the words of life.

Because we have tasted and seen that the Lord is good.

Because He loved us so much that He gave up His life for us.

Because we love Him.

Because we want to bring Him joy when we help another one of His children learn to love Him as much as we do.

How many more reasons do we really need?

Besides, the gospel was never really about saying a prayer so we could go to heaven—or escape hell—when we die. That's not the gospel that Jesus preached. It's not the gospel that the Apostles ever preached.

I'll admit, it was the gospel that I was raised hearing as a child. It was the Gospel I was trained to believe and to preach to others.

It wasn't until I was already a licensed and ordained minister of the gospel who had served for years in various Christians churches and denominations that I finally realized what the actual gospel of Jesus really was.

And I've never been the same since.

Want to know what the gospel is really all about? Let's talk about that in our next chapter.

CHAPTER 10

THE GOSPEL REDISCOVERED

"Do not suppose that the soul is punished for endless eons (apeirou aionas) in Tartarus. Very properly, the soul is not punished to gratify the revenge of the divinity, but for the sake of healing. But we say that the soul is punished for an aionion period (aionios) calling its life and its allotted period of punishment, its aeon."

—OLYMPIODORUS (495 TO 570 A.D.)

The gospel is literally translated as "good news." It's what Jesus came preaching in the Sermon on the Mount, it's what the Disciples preached, and it's what the later Apostles preached.

That gospel is found most clearly in the books we call "The Gospels" of Mathew, Mark and Luke, and in a slightly different form in the Gospel of John.

Here's the gospel that Jesus preached:

"I must preach the *good news of the kingdom of God* to the other towns also, because that is why I was sent." (Luke 4:43) [emphasis mine]

"The time has come," he said. "*The kingdom of God is near. Repent and believe the good news!*" (Mark 1:15) [emphasis mine]

"Jesus went through all the towns and villages, teaching in their synagogues, *preaching the good news of the kingdom* and healing every disease and sickness." (Matt 9:35) [emphasis mine]

"Jesus went throughout Galilee, teaching in their synagogues, *preaching the good news of the kingdom.*" (Matt 4:23) [emphasis mine]

This "good news of the kingdom of God" was simply this: "The kingdom of God is within you" (Luke 17:21), meaning that we can experience the rule and reign of God in our lives today without waiting until after we die.

So, the good news of the kingdom is a gospel for our life, today. It's not merely something that kicks in after we are dead.

Or, as Dallas Willard so eloquently phrased it:

"The gospel is less about how to get into the kingdom of heaven after you die, and more about how to live in the kingdom of heaven before you die."

For me, this epiphany reoriented my understanding of the entire Christian life. Suddenly, I understood that what Jesus wanted us to do was to enter into an actual experience with God right here and right now. It wasn't something we needed to wait for. It was something we could begin to explore immediately.

This caused me to rethink everything. It challenged my notions of discipleship, evangelism, fellowship, compassion, service, mercy, salvation, and pretty much every single element of my faith.

ONE FUNDAMENTAL SHIFT FOR ME WAS THE REALIZATION THAT THE GOSPEL WAS NOT PRIMARILY CONCERNED ABOUT GETTING ME INTO HEAVEN OR OUT OF HELL. INSTEAD, IT WAS MAINLY ABOUT THE IMPORTANCE OF FOLLOWING JESUS IN MY EVERYDAY LIFE.

In some ways, everything I've ever written or spoken about or experienced since that day has been reframed by this newfound understanding of the good news of the kingdom.

One fundamental shift for me was the realization that the gospel was not primarily concerned about getting me into heaven or out of hell. Instead, it was mainly about the importance of following Jesus in my everyday life.

So, rather than asking people if they knew they would be in heaven tomorrow if they were to die tonight, I started asking people a different question: "If you're alive tomorrow, who will you follow and how will you live your life?"

This is essentially what Jesus asked people when he looked at them and said, "Follow me!" Because discipleship—which is what being a Christian is all about—starts with this simple step: Following Jesus.

This is what it means to say that "Jesus is Lord," because we are putting his teachings into practice. This is primarily expressed by the way we live our lives; in obedience to Christ. It's not merely the speaking of the words—Jesus is Lord—as if it were some magic incantation that saves us when we repeat it out loud or put it on our bumper sticker. Not at all. What we're called to do is to actually, literally, truly live as though Christ is our Lord. How do we that? By taking up our cross daily. By dying to ourselves. By submitting our lives to Christ's kingship. When we do that, we are living as citizens of His kingdom. This is how we make it known to everyone around us that "Jesus Christ is Lord."

Now, I have to emphasize that this is not about doing good works to be saved. Not at all. I totally affirm that we are all saved by grace, as Paul stresses:

> "For by grace you have been saved through faith. And this is not your own doing; it is the gift of God, not a result of works, so that no one may boast." (Eph. 2:8-9)

So, we are totally, one hundred percent, saved by the grace of God. However, if we keep reading, we'll also notice this in the very next verse:

"For we are his workmanship, created in Christ Jesus to do good works, which God prepared beforehand, that we should walk in them." (Eph. 2:10)

See that? We are saved by grace to do good works. Or, as I prefer to phrase it:

"Swimming won't make you a fish. But if you're a fish, you will swim."

In other words, we don't do good works to be saved. But, if we are saved and transformed by the indwelling spirit of Christ, then we are certainly going to do the things that transformed people do: we're going to walk like Christ.

So, we are called to be like Jesus. That's not impossible. In fact, it's fundamental to being a follower of Jesus.

"This is how we know that we are in Him [Christ]: Whoever claims to live in him must walk as Jesus did." (1 John 2:5-6)

"His divine power has given us everything we need for life and godliness through our knowledge of him who called us....He has given us His very great and precious promises so that through them you may participate in the Divine nature." (1 Peter 1:3-4)

Unfortunately, another negative by product of a gospel that is merely about getting us out of hell and into heaven, is that we tend to deny the power of Christ or the grace of God to do anything more than save us. We start to emphasize our sinfulness and even to celebrate our inability to do the things that Jesus commands us to do all through the Gospels.

So, we tend to ignore passages like those I've shared above, and this one:

"For the grace of God has appeared, bringing salvation to all men…instructing us to deny ungodliness and worldly desires and to live sensibly, righteously and godly in the present age…" (Titus 2:11-12)

Yes, the first part of that passage affirms that the grace of God brings "salvation to all men", but we neglect to realize that this same grace of God goes on to instruct us "to deny ungodliness and worldly desires, and to live sensibly, righteously and godly *in the present age.*"

That's not about after we die. That's here and now.

But, how can we actually live like Christ? Isn't that impossible?

Alone, yes, it is impossible. We can't even come close to obeying the words of Jesus apart from His indwelling presence in our daily lives.

That's why Jesus said: *"Apart from me you can do nothing."* (John 15:5)

But what if we abide in Him? What if He abides in us? Then, and only then, can we *"bear much fruit."* (John 15:5)

This is why Jesus can promise us that his yoke is easy and his burden is light even as he calls us to do things that seem impossible, like love our enemies and forgive those who hurt us, and turn the other cheek.

How can Jesus say that? Because we're not expected to do it alone.

Remember, *"I can do all things through Christ who strengthens me"* (Phil. 4:13).

When Jesus says, *"Take my yoke upon you…"* (Matt 11:29) he's saying that He will be right beside us, all the way, and that we won't have to do everything in our own strength, but in His.

Yes, Jesus expects you to put His words into practice. He empowers you to do exactly that. He fills you with His Holy Spirit to enable you to do the things that He did.

All we have to do is to trust in Him and daily seek to allow Christ to live and breathe in us by His Spirit.

So let me encourage you today: if you are in Christ, you have everything you need to live a godly, Christ-like life right now!

"I have been crucified with Christ and I no longer live, but Christ lives in me. The life I now live in the body, I live by faith in the Son of God, who loved me and gave himself for me." (Galatians 2:20)

SO LET ME ENCOURAGE YOU TODAY: IF YOU ARE IN CHRIST, YOU HAVE EVERYTHING YOU NEED TO LIVE A GODLY, CHRIST-LIKE LIFE RIGHT NOW!

So, we can follow Jesus and we can put his words into practice daily. Sure, we may blow it now and again, but we don't give up, just like we don't encourage toddlers to stop trying to walk if they fall down once in a while. That's to be expected. But when we fall, we get back up, and we keep on walking in the path that Jesus has marked out for us to walk.

Even so, having said all of that, we probably need to answer another question that's related to this topic: "Is Jesus the only way to Heaven?"

That's our next chapter.

CHAPTER 11

JESUS IS "THE WAY" (TO WHAT?)

"Wherefore, that at the same time liberty of free will should be left to nature and yet the evil be purged away, the wisdom of God discovered this plan; to suffer man to do what he would, that having tasted the evil which he desired, and learning by experience for what wretchedness he had bartered away the blessings he had, he might of his own will hasten back with desire to the first blessedness…either being purged in this life through prayer and discipline, or after his departure hence through the furnace of cleansing fire."

—GREGORY OF NYSSA (332 TO 398 A.D.)

We hear this all the time: "Jesus is the only way to heaven" or "No one will be saved without knowing Jesus."

But is that true? Well, maybe, but that's not what Jesus meant when he said:

> "I am the way, and the truth, and the life. No one comes to the Father except through me…" (John 14:6)

I understand that most of us have been *told* that this is what Jesus means to say in this verse, but a careful study of the entire chapter reveals something a bit different.

First of all, this statement is in response to the question asked by Thomas, *"Lord, we do not know where you are going. How can we know the way?"*

That's why Jesus said, *"I am the way..."*

The way to where? *The way to where he is going.*

Where is Jesus going? *He's going to the Father.*

So, this entire chapter is about coming to the Father, not about going to Heaven after we die.

After this, Jesus goes on to explain that if you've seen him, you've also seen the Father. So, the entire point of the conversation is about knowing the Father.

WHY IS THAT IMPORTANT? BECAUSE THE WORKS THAT JESUS DOES ARE EVIDENCE THAT THE FATHER IS IN HIM. SO, THE WORKS THAT WE DO ARE ALSO EVIDENCE THAT JESUS—AND THE FATHER—ARE IN US.

And what is the evidence given to show us that the Father is in him, and that he is in the Father? His works.

Then notice that Jesus immediately pivots to emphasize that, if we trust in him, we will also do the same works he has been doing.

Why is that important? Because the works that Jesus does are evidence that the Father is in him. So, the works that we do are also evidence that Jesus—and the Father—are in us.

The whole conversation is about coming to the Father and what it means to be in Christ, and about Jesus going to "prepare a place for (us)", so that where Jesus is, we may also be.

So, if we keep reading in John 14 we will notice that Jesus reemphasizes this same idea over and over again:

"In that day you will know that I am in my Father, and you in me, and I in you." (v. 20)

"And I will ask the Father, and he will give you another Helper, to be with you forever, even the Spirit of truth, whom the world cannot receive, because it neither sees him nor knows

him. You know him, for he dwells with you and will be in you."
(v. 16-17)

The point is: Jesus is going to the Father. This is what he's talking about in the beginning of the chapter. The disciples get confused, so Jesus explains that he is going to the Father, and he is the way to the Father because the Father is in him, and the plan is for us to have the Father—and Jesus—living in us so that "where they are we may also be."

So, where is Jesus? *Jesus is with the Father.* (v. 12; 28)

And where is the Father? *He, and Jesus, have now come to make their home in you and in me.* (v. 23)

Notice that Jesus says in the previous chapter, *"Where I am going, you cannot follow now, but you will follow later."* (Jn. 13:36)

That's what sets up the conversation in chapter 14 about where Jesus is going and how we can also follow him to the place he is going (to be with the Father).

So, this idea of being with the Father, and abiding in Christ (who abides in us and in the Father), is something we can all experience *right now*!

We don't need to wait until after we die to be where Jesus and the Father are. In fact, this is the entire point of Jesus's going away! It was to prepare a place where we can be together with him and the Father.

Note: Jesus is *not* talking about where we go after we die. Jesus is talking about how we can know him—and the Father—*before* we die!

That's quite a significant difference.

So, to recap: Jesus is the way to know the Father. He is the truth about who the Father is, because if we've seen him we've also seen the Father. Jesus is our source for life—right here and now—as we abide in him, and he—and the Father—abide daily in us.

That's what Jesus is talking about in this verse. Not about where we go after we die, but about where Jesus and the Father go when we abide in them *before* we die.

But, what if it's about more than just knowing God? What if it was also about God knowing us?

I know, I know. God is omniscient, right? So, obviously, God already knows me, because God knows everyone. But, if that's the case, what do we do with verses like this one?

> "But now that you have come to know God, or rather *to be known by God*, how is it that you turn back again to the weak and worthless elemental things, to which you desire to be enslaved all over again?" (Gal. 4:9) [emphasis mine]

Notice that Paul starts to say that we have come to know God—which sort of lines up with our theology—but then he does something kind of strange; he backtracks and corrects himself and then says, *"or rather to be known by God"*, which is a little odd.

I mean, how can God not already know everyone and everything, right? Doesn't God already know everything that could ever be known?

Well, if that's true, then what does Paul mean when he stops himself from talking about the importance of "knowing God" and clarifies that what he actually means to say is that we should be "known by God"?

Well, before you answer that, maybe you should look at this other verse where Paul sort of does it again:

> "If anyone supposes that he knows anything, he has not yet known as he ought to know; but if anyone loves God, *he is known by Him*." (1 Cor. 8:2) [emphasis mine]

Look at that. Paul, once more, emphasizes that the one who "supposes that he knows" actually "has not yet known as he ought to know"—which kind of starts to sound like Paul isn't all that impressed by "knowing" God, or theology, or information.

Maybe this does make sense. Especially if you start to look at other places where Paul says that he considers all the religious knowledge and learning he once had as a Pharisee to be rubbish, or dung, compared to knowing Christ. He even went so far as to say that he resolved to know *nothing* other than Christ.

So, maybe what Paul has in mind is closer to a relationship with another person—one where you know them and they know you, intimately.

See, nowadays, Christians tend to have an idea that their faith is more about knowing stuff *about* God, and that usually means they tend to downplay *knowing God*.

Now, before you get upset at me for saying this, let me assure you that I have been told many, many times by dozens (maybe hundreds) of Christians over the last few years that it is more important to know the right stuff about God than to know God. Not only that, they usually go the extra mile to assure me that it is pretty much impossible to know God in any actual, intimate, relational way other than knowing the information about God that is printed in their Bible.

KNOWING STUFF ABOUT GOD IS NOT WHAT IT'S ALL ABOUT. ALLOWING GOD TO KNOW YOU IS WHAT REALLY MATTERS.

But Paul totally contradicts this notion. He actually says the exact opposite: Knowing stuff about God is not what it's all about. Allowing God to *know you* is what really matters.

What's the difference? Well, for example, I could know all sorts of trivia about Michael Jordan. I could find out his favorite color, his birthdate, the name of his first dog, what elementary school he went to, his favorite ice cream, etc. and eventually I could become the world's leading authority on Michael Jordan. But, even if I did all of that, and I bumped into Michael Jordan at the grocery store, he would not say, "Oh, hey Keith! How are you doing?"

Why? Because, even though I know all sorts of *information* about Michael Jordan, I do not *know* Michael Jordan. Why? Because Michael Jordan does not know me.

It's the same with Jesus. I could know all sorts of information about Jesus, but that does not mean that I know Jesus. Or that Jesus knows me.

Want proof? Try this:

> "Not everyone who says to me, 'Lord, Lord,' will enter the kingdom of heaven, but the one who does the will of my Father who is in heaven. On that day many will say to me, 'Lord, Lord, did we not prophesy in your name, and cast out demons in your name, and do many mighty works in your name?' And then will I declare to them, '*I never knew you*; depart from me, you workers of lawlessness.'" (Matt. 7:21-23) [emphasis mine]

See? It is more than possible to not only know all sorts of stuff *about* Jesus but to even do amazing works *for* Jesus and in the *name* of Jesus, without really allowing Jesus to *know you*.

So, what do we do about this? How can we make sure that we know Jesus and that Jesus knows us?

Maybe we should start by being still. Maybe we need to sit down in a quiet place and close our eyes and listen for that still, small voice of God.

Maybe we need to learn how to talk to God, and more importantly, how to listen for God's voice.

I want us to go back and look again at the verse where Paul says:

> "If anyone supposes that he knows anything, he has not yet known as he ought to know; but if anyone loves God, *he is known by Him*." (1 Cor. 8:2) [emphasis mine]

Notice that Paul emphasizes the need to love God? It's not about knowing stuff. That has nothing to do with love, does it? As I said earlier, I could know everything about Michael Jordan but still not love Michael Jordan—especially if I had never met him.

We need to meet the object of our love.

We need to spend time with the one we love.

We need to learn to fall in love with God, truly and sincerely.

So, let go of your doctrines. Let go of your information. Stop trying to know stuff about God and start allowing God to know you.

Go back and read that verse one last time: *"If anyone supposes that he knows anything, he has not yet known as he ought to know…"* Does that describe you? Do you suppose that you know things about God? Are you the wise teacher who feels the need to instruct everyone else around you? If so, please consider Paul's words here: Maybe you have not yet known as you ought to know. Maybe the kind of "knowing" you have achieved so far is just the ordinary "knowing" of information. Maybe it's time to re-think what it means to "know" and to embrace the wisdom of "being known by Him."

Maybe it's time to stop focusing on your doctrines and let go of acquiring information. Instead of storing up knowledge about God, maybe it's time to allow God to *know you.*

Let's remember that God is love. So, if that's true, then let's start by learning to love God. Why? Because *"the only thing that counts is faith expressing itself through love"* (Gal. 5:6), and because Jesus says that *"if anyone loves me…my Father will love him and we will come to him and make our home in him."* (John 14:23)

This is what the Gospel is really all about: knowing God, and being known by God intimately enough to allow this new life to be formed within us. It is more about life than afterlife; more being known than knowing things; more transformation than information.

All of this makes more sense when you stop to realize that God is love, and love is meant to be experienced.

CHAPTER 12

WHAT COMES NEXT?

"That in the world to come, those who have done evil all their life long, will be made worthy of the sweetness of the Divine bounty. For never would Christ have said, "You will never get out until you have paid the last penny" unless it were possible for us to get cleansed when we paid the debt."

—PETER CHRYSOLOGUS, (380 TO 450 A.D.)

When it comes to the afterlife, the Bible is surprisingly vague. Most of our ideas about where we go and what happens to us after we die come from tradition, religious folklore, and medieval literature, not from the Bible itself.

If we do look to the Old Testament for answers, we only find references to the grave—Sheol, or Hades, literally the place of the dead—but no actual details of what happens to us there.

If we look to the New Testament for insights, we only find references to Gehenna—literally the Valley of Hinnom outside the walls of Jerusalem—and those verses (as we have already seen) are not about where we go after we die, but are apocalyptic warnings to first century Jews about the coming destruction of Jerusalem which was fulfilled in 70 AD.

We also see a few metaphorical images of the Lake of Fire in Revelation, and Jesus tells us a parable that was common to the culture of his day about a rich man and a poor man who both die and experience a reversal of fortune in the afterlife. But this is more of a warning for us to honor the poor in this life or risk suffering for our lack of compassion in the next. We should not take that parable as a description of what happens to us after we die.

What's fascinating is how similar the parable of the Rich Man and Lazarus, which Jesus re-tells in the Gospel of Luke, mirrors the message of Matthew 25:40 where Jesus rewards those who were kind to the poor and the marginalized but rebukes those who were unkind to them. The moral and theme of this passage is almost exactly the same moral and message found in the parable: Those who do not share their wealth with the poor in this life will have to give an account for their lack of charity in the next life.

For that reason, perhaps both of these passages are meant to serve more as parables to us about our need to love one another as Christ has loved us and less as depictions of what will happen to us after we die.

Still, if the Matthew 25 passage is intended to teach us about the afterlife, it's quite vague. What we see in this passage, and in a few others within the New Testament is simply this: We all die, and we all face some form of judgement for our behaviors in this life. From here the path may take several possible turns. We may be tested in the fire and proven true, or found wanting. But either way, according to 1 Cor. 3:15, we *"will be saved as those who pass through the fire."* Or, as in Matthew 25:26, we may be found unrighteous and suffer endless punishment.

But which is it? Do we suffer for eternity? Or do we pass through the fire and enjoy another opportunity to receive the boundless saving grace of Christ? Or do we endure a period of suffering and then cease to exist?

The answer is: "Yes."

In other words, if you're looking for a handful of Bible verses that support one of those three views, you can certainly find them. We've already examined those verses in great detail. What we've found is that a lot of verses that seem to be about hell are not at all about where we go or what happens to us after we die. We've also seen that metaphors and parables get treated like literal events, and what we notice is that the Biblical authors don't seem to be as interested in what happens to us after we die as we seem to be today.

As my friend, and Bible Scholar, Steve Gregg noted in an email to me recently:

> "It does seem as if the mention of the afterlife is entirely absent from the Old Testament, and barely visible in the New Testament. I am under the impression that references to "immortality" have impact on the subject, but they obviously do nothing to satisfy human curiosity about the nature of things in postmortem existence. My impression is that the afterlife was simply not the front-burner issue in the early church that it seems to be in subsequent Christendom."[1]

So, what it may come down to is this: which of these three views is more closely aligned with the character of God as revealed to us through Christ?

If we see God as being too holy to look upon our wretched sinfulness, then we may require a version of hell that accommodates this view of God.

But, if we see God as the "Abba" that Jesus revealed to us, then we may reject notions of a God who could torture His children for eternity and withhold His mercy from them forever. Instead, we may decide that God is like a Father whose primary posture towards us is love and who will do whatever it takes to redeem us and restore us to fellowship as beloved children.

Yes, we may embrace this because God is love, and no one would ever be a better Father than God is.

But, some may caution us, what about God's wrath?

Why don't we examine that in our next chapter?

CHAPTER 13

GOD OF WRATH?

"In the liberation of all no one remains a captive! At the time of the Lord's passion the devil alone was injured by losing all the of the captives he was keeping."

—DIDYMUS, (370 AD)

Whenever we point out that God is love, it's not uncommon to hear at least one person chime in and say: "But God is also a god of wrath!"

Is that true? I mean, we do have one verse in the Bible that tells us that God actually *is* love:

"Whoever does not love does not know God, because God is love." (1 John 4:8)

I think it's worth noting that, while we do find verses that speak about the wrath of God, we do not find any verses that say "God *is* wrath."

That, to me, is significant. So, if we ever read any verses that talk about the wrath of God, or the judgment of God, or anything else, we need to always filter that through the understanding that God is love. That means that

THE WRATH OF GOD IS ALWAYS UNDERSTOOD THROUGH THE REALIZATION THAT GOD IS LOVE.

the wrath of God is always understood through the realization that God is love. Another way to phrase it might be to say: "The wrath of the God who is love," or "The wrath of a loving God."

My friend Steve Kline recently shared his thoughts on this in one of his blog posts inspired by something he noticed in Psalm 18:25-27 which says:

> "With the merciful you show yourself merciful; with the blameless you show yourself blameless; with the purified you show yourself pure; and with the crooked you make yourself seem tortuous." (Psalm 18:25-27)

Here's what Steve took from this passage:

> "The conception among most Christians is that God is angry with us and that if we don't repent then He will pour out His wrath on us…Yes, we have sinned horribly against God. We denied him…For that, we must repent if we want to enter the kingdom of God, the kingdom of heaven, eternal life.

> "…But, for those that don't repent, is it God's wrath that will be poured out on them? Or, is it the lies and the violence of the unrepentant themselves that will come back on their own head? Throughout the Bible, we see that the pit the wicked dug they themselves fall into. Or, the snare that evil people set they get caught in themselves. And, in the depictions of Satan (for example, Goliath and Haman), he is almost always killed with his own weapon."

> "The repentant have become merciful, blameless, and purified. And, to the repentant God shows Himself as such. But, to the unrepentant, the crooked (in Psalm 18), God makes Himself seem tortuous. It seems to them like God is vengeful, spiteful, and vindictive, pouring His wrath out on them. However, in reality, it is their own lies and violence that are coming back on their own heads."[1]

This is a key insight—from the Scriptures—that we need to take seriously. The wrath of God is quite often something experienced as the fruit of one's own actions rather than as the direct action of God against the unrighteous.

I believe this is exactly what's happening all throughout the ministry of Jesus. He arrives on the scene and warns the people to repent—to literally think differently and start to live a different sort of life—or else they will suffer the consequences of their actions.

Specifically, the Jewish people in the first century were longing for a Messiah to come and liberate them from the tyranny and rule of the Romans. That mindset is eventually what led them to suffer the total destruction of Jerusalem, their temple, the priesthood, and the end of life as they knew it.

This is what Jesus is trying to warn them about over and over again:

> "You have heard that it was said, 'An eye for an eye and a tooth for a tooth.' But I tell you not to resist an evil person. But whoever slaps you on your right cheek, turn the other to him also. If anyone wants to sue you and take away your tunic, let him have your cloak also. And whoever compels you to go one mile, go with him two. Give to him who asks you, and from him who wants to borrow from you do not turn away.

> "You have heard that it was said, 'You shall love your neighbor and hate your enemy.' But I say to you, love your enemies, bless those who curse you, do good to those who hate you, and pray for those who spitefully use you and persecute you, that you may be sons of your Father in heaven; for He makes His sun rise on the evil and on the good, and sends rain on the just and on the unjust. For if you love those who love you, what reward have you? Do not even the tax collectors do the same? And if you greet your brethren only, what do you do more than others? Do not even the tax collectors do so? Therefore you shall be perfect, just as your Father in heaven is perfect." (Matt. 5:38-48)

> "Therefore whoever hears these sayings of Mine, and does them, I will liken him to a wise man who built his house on

the rock: and the rain descended, the floods came, and the winds blew and beat on that house; and it did not fall, for it was founded on the rock.

"But everyone who hears these sayings of Mine, and does not do them, will be like a foolish man who built his house on the sand: and the rain descended, the floods came, and the winds blew and beat on that house; and it fell. And great was its fall." (Matt. 7:24-27)

In the same way, the prophecy spoken by Jesus in the Olivet Discourse (see Matt. 24) is another example of the wrath of God that was prophesied by Jesus but fulfilled by the Roman army that surrounded Jerusalem and destroyed it, just as Jesus said they would.

But, this destruction was specifically in retaliation for an armed rebellion against the Roman Empire; something that Jesus urged them to repent of by following his teachings about loving their enemies and blessing those who curse them.

This sowing and reaping, or cause-and-effect scenario is played out all through the Gospels. But just because Jesus uses apocalyptic language and warns his people that they face the "wrath of God" for refusing to put his teachings into practice, it does not mean that God is personally responsible for the destruction. In fact, it's the exact opposite. God sent Jesus as a prophet to warn His people about their need to stop seeking to overthrow the Romans. Jesus told them exactly what would happen if they refused to take another approach—love their enemies, bless them, do good to them, walk the extra mile, turn the other cheek, etc.

So, this preaching was an expression of the love of God and the compassion of God to His people, not an expression of God's wrath. The goal of Christ's message was to save them from this destructive way of living.

Unfortunately, only a few people took this new approach to heart. Those who did were saved from this destruction, but those who did not listen to Jesus were not spared the fruit of their rebellious behavior. This was not an example of God's wrath or punishment as much as it was the effect of reaping what they, themselves, had sown in defiance of Christ's message.

The wrath of God, therefore, appears to be more about suffering the consequences of our own actions and less about the anger of God being expressed directly against the wicked.

THE WRATH OF GOD, THEREFORE, APPEARS TO BE MORE ABOUT SUFFERING THE CONSEQUENCES OF OUR OWN ACTIONS AND LESS ABOUT THE ANGER OF GOD BEING EXPRESSED DIRECTLY AGAINST THE WICKED.

What we see is that God—who is love—always works to warn us about these disastrous consequences. Because God loves us, His hope is that we will choose another path which will lead us to life and away from destruction.

In fact, the overarching sweep of the Scripture is that God's posture towards us is always good. As Steve Gregg puts it:

> "None of God's actions, including His judgments, are without a positive purpose. This is often affirmed in Scripture...Since there are many such [verses] that speak of God's judging as a function of His love and mercy—while there are none that tell us that God's judgments are merely retributive...it seems inappropriate and gratuitous to interpret the few verses in Scripture about hell as if we did not have ample testimony elsewhere revealing the divine purpose and intention of saving all that were lost."[2]

Again, we can affirm the scriptures which reveal to us the truth that "God is love," and we can see—through the living example of Jesus—that God is *not* a God of wrath. He's a God who loves us enough to warn us when our actions are leading us to destruction and he weeps for us when we fail to see the things that make for peace.

So, when we see phrases like the "wrath of the Lamb" in scripture, as in Revelation 6:16, we have to stop and ask ourselves what is really being described.

As my friend Richard Murray notes:

"Jesus is the Lamb of God. So He, by extension, is the wrath of God personified [in Revelation 6:16]. But here is the thing: Lambs have no wrath.

"So, the term is an oxymoron. It's an image clash where wrath itself is deconstructed by the jarring contradiction of two incompatible terms. This then allows divine wrath to be conceptually recast as the restorative and curative energies of God. Hence the Lamb.

"So let's look at both God's birth statement and death statement regarding Jesus as the revelation of 'the wrath of God.'

"Here is the divine wrath statement given by angelic pronouncement at His birth: 'Peace on earth, goodwill to man.' (Luke 2:14) Hmmm.

"And here is His bookend statement on the issue of wrath at His death: 'Forgive them Father, for they know not what they do.' (Luke 23:34) Hmmm.

"The 'wrath of the Lamb' is now revealed. Peace, goodwill, and forgiveness toward all men!"[3]

This same oxymoron is further exemplified in David Bentley Hart's translation of the New Testament where he notes that the "Lamb" in Revelation 5:6 is more accurately rendered as "The suckling lamb", which is the equivalent of a kitten or a newborn puppy.

As he puts it:

"Not *arnos* or *arnen*—a "lamb"—but an *arnion*—literally, a "little lamb" or "lambkin", a term most properly applied to a lamb that is still nursing."[4]

So, this image of Christ as the "suckling lamb" or "newborn lambkin" further challenges the notion that the "wrath of the Lamb" is anything other than an intentionally jarring mashup of clashing ideas that lead us to rethink our notions of the wrath of God.

> **WHAT WE KNOW IS THIS: GOD'S PLAN AND PURPOSE IS ALWAYS TO RESTORE US, REDEEM US, RENEW US AND HEAL US. GOD'S ULTIMATE PURPOSE IS NEVER TO HURT US, HARM US OR DESTROY US.**

What we know is this: God's plan and purpose is always to restore us, redeem us, renew us and heal us. God's ultimate purpose is never to hurt us, harm us or destroy us. That is what Jesus told us that our enemy came to do, but Jesus said his mission was to undo all of that once and for all (see John 10:10-29; 1 John 3:8).

"We must die. But that is not what God desires; rather, he devises ways so that a banished person does not remain banished from him." (2 Sam. 14:14)

God is love. God is not wrath. God is not judgment. God is exactly like Jesus who freely forgives us and heals us. His love endures forever. And it's the kindness of God that leads us all to repentance.

If wrath and vengeance were truly attributes of God's character and reflections of His Divine Nature, then we might expect to see these listed alongside the other Fruits of the Spirit found in the Scriptures.

After all, the Fruit of the Spirit is simply a reflection of the nature and character of God imparted to us by the Holy Spirit as we abide in Christ. These attributes—love, joy, peace, patience, kindness, gentleness and self-control—are Divine attributes. We bear these fruits because we are being transformed by the Spirit of God into people who reflect the image and nature of God as revealed in Christ.

Wrath is not an attribute of God's nature. Vengeance is not a reflection of God's heart.

What we see in the Suckling Lamb is the true face of God who is not wrathful, but loving and merciful.

CHAPTER 14

THE FRUIT OF UNIVERSALISM

"Our Lord descends, and was shut up in the eternal bars, in order that He might set free all who had been shut up... The Lord descended to the place of punishment and torment, in which was the rich man, in order to liberate the prisoners."

—JEROME (347 TO 420 A.D.)

The more I've studied the doctrine of Universal Reconciliation, the more I've started to notice something about those who embrace the view: they tend to be more loving and accepting of those who are unlike them.

Maybe it's because when you realize that everyone is equally loved by God, and that God is really intending to bring everyone to repentance, and that, one day, every knee will bow and every tongue will *gladly* confess that Jesus Christ is Lord, well, you kind of relax and enjoy being alive.

See, instead of seeing people as "saved" or "lost," and grouping everyone you meet into the "Christian" or "non-Christian" category, you may start to see people as simply people.

Not only that, but you also begin to see them as God sees them. You slowly recognize that everyone you meet—regardless of their beliefs or spiritual condition—is someone who is dearly loved by God. You also start to understand that everyone you meet is indeed your brother or sister, and you realize that we all have the same Heavenly Father.

This really starts to change the way you treat other people. It starts to bear good fruit in your life. It even makes it easier to love others as Christ has loved you, without conditions or strings attached.

Eventually, you begin to recognize that God loves everyone much more than you could ever love them; even your own family members who may be far from faith in Christ at the moment. You start to realize that God has a grand design in motion to draw everyone to Himself, eventually. We get to take part in that, if we can learn to abide in Christ and collaborate with the Holy Spirit in this process. But, we can also enjoy a newfound sense of ease with this process. Because now we're not fighting the clock or worried about closing the sale. Instead, we're trusting in God's ultimate victory which is inevitable and unstoppable.

UNFORTUNATELY, SOME CHRISTIANS DON'T SEE THIS. THEY'RE CONVINCED THAT GOD IS MORE COSMIC JUDGE THAN ABBA FATHER. IN FACT, THEY'RE MORE OFFENDED BY THE IDEA THAT GOD WILL SAVE EVERYONE THAN THEY ARE THAT GOD MIGHT BURN THE MAJORITY OF PEOPLE FOR ETERNITY.

Unfortunately, some Christians don't see this. They're convinced that God is more cosmic judge than Abba Father. In fact, they're more offended by the idea that God will save everyone than they are that God might burn the majority of people for eternity.

That boggles the mind. I can understand it, in some odd way, only because at one time I held that belief about God. But now I can't reconcile this with what I see of the Father's heart revealed to us by Jesus.

One fascinating thing I've discovered as I've studied this subject is *why* those early Christian teachers taught this doctrine of Eternal Suffering.

Their stated reason for embracing this minority view were quite simply this: Fear.

Yes, fear, they found, was very effective in evangelism, and this same fear of eternal torment also helped to keep people in line.

For example, two of those pre-Augustine Church Fathers who preached an eternal Hell were Basil and John Chrysostrom. Here's a bit about why they valued the doctrine of Eternal Suffering:

"Brian Edward Daley, in *The Hope of the Early Church*, remarks that Basil was "an admirer of Origen in his younger days" and was closely familiar with his work. However, in his later years he became "more severe in his own expectations of the future" and *found the teaching of judgment valuable for the spiritual development of Christians.*"[1] [emphasis mine]

"Like Basil, Chrysostom saw eschatological themes as a crucial part of his preaching ministry...Chrysostom explains the need for such eternal punishment elsewhere. For example, in his 15th homily on 1 Timothy, he emphasizes the value of fear in constraining sin:

"Since the greater part are virtuous from constraint rather than from choice, *the principle of fear is of great advantage to them in eradicating their desires. Let us therefore listen to the threatenings of hell fire, that we may be benefited by the wholesome fear of it.*"[2] [emphasis mine]

I shouldn't have to say this, but fear and control are poor reasons for embracing and promoting a doctrine. Especially when we have the advantage of seeing what a few hundred year's worth of this teaching can do to people's faith.

Today, hundreds of thousands, perhaps millions, of people have abandoned the Christian faith over this doctrine which portrays God as a vengeful, wrathful Deity who cannot love or forgive unless there is blood spilled and a sacrifice made. Many others have avoided the Christian faith completely for the very same reason.

What's worse is when you realize that such an offensive doctrine has very little scriptural support. As we've seen, most of the verses that are referenced to bolster this view of the tormenting God are either using apocalyptic language from the Old Covenant prophets—which were never about actual eternal worms, or fire, or smoke, but always about literal armies that would come to invade a city or a nation—or are verses that speak of "death" or "destruction," not about being eternally conscious to experience the fires of Hell.

Of the three views, I believe that only Annihilation and Universalism have any real legs to stand on; and neither of those two views paints God as a monster who requires blood and sacrifice, or who tortures his enemies endlessly and without mercy.

Personally, I have found that abandoning this primitive and false doctrine of Eternal Suffering leads to a changed perspective about your fellow man, and about the God that is revealed to us in Christ.

Studying this topic has been very encouraging for me, and I know that being set free from the fear of endless torment can really do wonders for your view of God, and your love for your fellow man.

I think it's time to forsake the false doctrine of Eternal Suffering and embrace the God who has "reconciled the world to Himself, not counting our sins against us" (2 Cor. 5:19).

Don't you?

CHAPTER 15

BETTER THAN WE THINK

"All men are Christ's, some by knowing Him, the rest not yet. He is the Savior, not of some and the rest not. For how is He Savior and Lord, if not the Savior and Lord of all?"

—CLEMENT OF ALEXANDRIA, (150 TO 215 A.D.)

Before we go any further, I'd like to get back to a few loose ends we left dangling in the book of Revelation a bit earlier in the book.

If you remember, we were looking at the language in chapter 20 of Revelation that talked about the wicked who were resurrected from the earth and the sea and brought before the throne of God's judgement. Then, in chapter 21, we looked at the New Jerusalem coming down out of Heaven and discovered that a lot of what was being talked about was actually already fulfilled by the Church which became the new Temple of God on earth.

There were a few other details I wanted to go back and look at, in light of all we've uncovered so far. For example, in Revelation 21, after John tells us about the Bride of Christ (that's the Church) which comes down out of Heaven as the New Jerusalem, we read these interesting words:

"He who was seated on the throne said, 'I am making every-thing new!'" (v. 5)

What makes this interesting is that it corresponds with Isaiah 65 which contains a Messianic prophecy about how nothing will ever be the same again.

God makes this promise in Isaiah 65:17 when He says:

"See, I will create new heavens and a new earth. The former things will not be remembered, nor will they come to mind."

What follows is a long list of contrasts between the way things are, and the way things will be after the Messiah comes: If there was death, there will be life. If there was violence, there will be peace. If there was despair, there will be hope.

In short, Jesus changes everything.

Best of all, the Messianic promise includes the renewal of humankind itself. So, not only will God make all *things* new, He will make all *people* new, as He says through Ezekiel:

"I will give you a new heart and put a new spirit in you; I will remove from you your heart of stone and give you a heart of flesh." (Ezekiel 36:26)

The reason why we are made new is so that we can contain the new life of Christ within, or as Jesus phrases it:

"People don't pour new wine into old wineskins. If they do, the skins will burst; the wine will run out and the wineskins will be ruined. No, they pour new wine into new wineskins, and both are preserved." (Matt. 9:17)

This means we need to be made new so we can receive the spirit of renewal within. We become agents of the new order; carriers of the renewal; catalysts of the resurrection.

This is why Paul says:

"Therefore, if anyone is in Christ, the new creation has come: The old has gone, the new is here!" (2 Cor. 5:17)

Sometimes I doubt we really grasp the magnitude of this statement. The old creation has faded away. There is now, literally, a new heaven and a new earth and a new humanity unleashed upon us.

Elsewhere, Paul says that we who are in Christ are taking off the old self in order to:

> "...be made new in the attitude of your minds; and to put on the new self, created to be like God in true righteousness and holiness." (Eph. 4:23-24)

This is God's entire plan: to remake the world from within, the way a small pinch of yeast spreads to transform the entire lump of dough and slowly causes it to rise.

As John describes it in Revelation, when the Bride of Christ—that's us—unites with Jesus here on Earth, everything begins to change. He and the Father come to make their home in us. Together, we experience the promise of the New Covenant where God's dwelling is now among us, and where He is our God, and we are His people.

From this divine/human connection, God shouts "I am making everything new!" (Rev. 21:5)

This genetic transformation has already begun. We are the new wineskins that are filled with the new wine. We are the new generation of the resurrection of Christ. We are the New Jerusalem that has come down from God out of Heaven. We are the new temple of God where Christ lives by His Spirit. We are the Body of Christ walking around in the world today. We are children of God that all creation eagerly anticipates.

THIS GENETIC TRANSFORMATION HAS ALREADY BEGUN. WE ARE THE NEW WINESKINS THAT ARE FILLED WITH THE NEW WINE. WE ARE THE NEW GENERATION OF THE RESURRECTION OF CHRIST. WE ARE THE NEW JERUSALEM THAT HAS COME DOWN FROM GOD OUT OF HEAVEN.

"For the creation waits with eager longing for the revealing of the sons of God." (Romans 8:19)

Because Jesus, our Messiah, has come, nothing—and no one—will ever be the same again.

But there's more.

The picture painted for us about the fate of the wicked and the righteous alike is told in rich metaphor between Revelation chapters 20 through 22. There's too much to quote here without essentially reprinting the entire thing, but here are the essential details we can see if we look closely:

- The wicked are in the lake of fire. (Rev. 20:15; 21:8)

- They are outside the gates of New Jerusalem. (Rev. 22:14-15)

- *Note: This mirrors the location of Gehenna in the Old Jerusalem where the "Lake of Fire" is just outside the gates of the city.

- The "nations of the earth" are the enemies who opposed Christ. (Rev. 20:3, 7)

- They are not allowed inside the New Jerusalem. (Rev. 21:27)

- But then we see a river of living water—waters of life—flowing from the center of the city where the throne of the Lamb is. (Rev. 22:1)

- All who are thirsty are invited to come and drink freely from these living waters/waters of life. (Rev. 21:6; 22:17)

- The gates of the city are always open and will never be shut. (Rev. 21:25)

- Those who "wash their robes may have the right to eat of the tree of life and go through the gates of the city." (Rev. 22:14)

- The tree of life bears fruit constantly—every month—and the leaves are for the "healing of the nations" who are outside the gates of the city. (Rev. 22:2)

- "The nations will walk by the light of the glory of God and the Lamb and the kings of the earth will bring their splendor into the city." (Rev. 21:23-24; 26)

- Only those whose names are written in the Lamb's book of life will enter the city. (Rev. 21:27)

So, what is the overall picture that is painted for us here? The wicked, the nations of the earth who were deceived by Satan, are judged, cast into the lake of fire which is outside the gates of the city of New Jerusalem. The city has gates that are never shut. The only light is the glory of God and the Lamb from within the city and the nations and the kings of the earth will walk in that light. Nothing impure is allowed inside the city, and yet those who are thirsty—perhaps suffering in the flames outside the city gates—are invited to come and drink freely from those waters of life that flow from the center of the throne of God and the Lamb, where the Tree of Life sprouts fruit every month and bears leaves that are specifically designed to heal the very same nations who are outside the city gates.

If no one whose name is not found in the Lamb's book of life is ever allowed to enter the city, then why are the gates always open?

Why is there an invitation for any who are thirsty to come and drink freely from those waters of life?

Why does it say that the "kings of the earth will bring their splendor into" this city if those kings are in the lake of fire outside the city gates?

Why does the Tree of Life bear leaves intended to heal the nations if those nations are the wicked who are in the lake of fire?

If the Spirit and the Bride say, "Come!" in Revelation 22:17 and then add, "Whoever is thirsty, let him come: and whoever wishes let him take the free gift of the water of life"; who are they talking to? Not to Jesus. He gives the very same invitation in verse 14. Not to the Church, because the Bride here *is* the Church.

The only other group of people being invited to come and drink the water of life—the only group of people not already inside the city gates—are those who are outside the city; the wicked, the nations who fought against Christ, and the kings of the earth who opposed the Lamb.

Is this why the gates are never shut? Is this why the light of Christ shines constantly from the center of the throne within the city? Is this why the Tree of Life bears fruit without end, every single month? Is this why the leaves of that glorious tree have only one purpose: to heal those nations who are outside the gates?

Consider this: The prophet Jeremiah says that the valley of Gehenna "will be holy to the Lord" (Jer. 31:40) and the Psalmist says that "..while thirsty hearts journey to appear before God in Zion, the valley of Gehenna will become a place of springs" (Ps. 84:5-7).

Notice that in Revelation 22:3 it says this: "No longer will there be any curse."

Sin will be finally dealt with. Not tortured forever. Not disintegrated. Redeemed.

"Behold!" says the Lamb of God. "I am making everything new!"

And every knee will bow. And every tongue will *gladly* confess, "Jesus! You are Lord!" to the glory of God the Father.

Hallelujah! Amen!

And the Spirit and the Bride say, "Amen!"

CHAPTER 16

ALL MADE NEW

"God forbid that I should limit the time of acquiring faith to the present life. In the depth of the Divine mercy there may be opportunity to win it in the future."

—MARTIN LUTHER (LETTER TO HANSEU VON RECHENBERG, 1522)

As wonderful as all of this may be—and I do believe it is even more wonderful than we can conceive—you may find yourself with a few unanswered questions.

Such as, "How does all of this work out in the here and now?" and "What are we waiting for if these end times prophecies in Revelation are actually already fulfilled in Christ and the Church today?"

If the dwelling place of God is now among men, as we read in Revelation 21:3, then the rivers of living water that flow from the center of the new city, or the new temple, are the same living waters that Jesus said would flow out of us—His people—His Body—His Temple—in the Gospel of John:

"If anyone thirsts, let him come to me and drink. Whoever believes in me, as the Scripture has said, 'Out of his heart will flow rivers of living water.'" (John 7:37-38)

"Whoever drinks the water I give them will never thirst. Indeed, the water I give them will become in them a spring of water welling up to eternal life." (John 4:14)

On one level, we all claim to affirm this. We say we understand that these realities are spiritually true already, right now. And yet we also, at the same time, continue to wait for God to "fulfill" these prophecies literally. As if to fulfill them literally would accomplish something new, or different from what we are experiencing today.

> **THE REAL PROBLEM IS THIS: SINCE WE MAY NOT ALWAYS EXPERIENCE THESE THINGS AS REALITIES RIGHT NOW, WE ACT AS IF THE SPIRITUAL FULFILLMENT OF THESE THINGS IS LIKE SOME SECOND-RATE CONSOLATION PRIZE.**

The real problem is this: since we may not always experience these things as realities right now, we act as if the spiritual fulfillment of these things is like some second-rate consolation prize. We can't help but think that one day, when God really shows up and makes it literally happen in front of our eyes, then it will finally "come true."

But that's not the way it works, I'm afraid.

The reality is Christ. He has come. He has fulfilled those types and shadows. The old has gone. The new has come.

We are told that those literal things—the temple, the priesthood, the daily sacrifice—were the shadow of what was to come, and now that the reality is here—Christ. Those shadows have vanished and are already fading away and have become obsolete (see Colossians 2:17; Hebrews 10:1).

See, there will never be any greater reality than Christ. For us, the fulfillment of a new creation has already come to pass. The New Covenant proclaimed by Jesus in the upper room has now been inaugurated and fulfilled nearly 2,000 years ago.

All that's left is for us to wake up and realize that it's true: We are now living in the New Heavens and the New Earth that God promised us so long ago.

The Divine has come to touch the earth. The seed was planted. The fruit has begun to ripen. Nothing will ever be the same again.

We are the New Jerusalem. We are the end times temple. We are the Body of Jesus—literally the new Incarnation of Christ in the world today. We are the stewards of His living water that now flows from within, and, along with the Holy Spirit, we are calling out to those outside the gates who are thirsty: "Come and drink freely from the waters of life!"

Let Christ arise and awaken from within. He is alive! He is reigning from His throne! His Kingdom has come!

This is not something we need to wait for. It's not "going to happen." It has already happened—and continues to happen— every single day!

This truth bears fruit like a tree of life that constantly produces good things every month of the year.

No, these gates will never be shut. Yes, this invitation is always open, and this offer never expires.

Come and drink freely. Come and be healed. Come and see that all things are being made new—including you.

Hallelujah! Long live the King!

Jesus is victorious. Every knee shall bow. Every tongue shall *gladly* confess. Christ is Lord of all.

He is now, and was, and forever will be, undefeated.

QUOTATIONS BY EARLY CHURCH FATHERS ON UNIVERSALISM

"The mass of men (Christians) say there is to be an end to punishment and to those who are punished."
—St. Basil the Great (329 to 379 A.D.)

"There are very many in our day, who though not denying the Holy Scriptures, do not believe in endless torments."
—Augustine (354 to 430 A.D.)

"For the wicked there are punishments, not perpetual, however, lest the immortality prepared for them should be a disadvantage, but they are to be purified for a brief period according to the amount of malice in their works. They shall therefore suffer punishment for a short space, but immortal blessedness having no end awaits them...the penalties to be inflicted for their many and grave sins are very far surpassed by the magnitude of the mercy to be showed to them."
—Diodore of Tarsus (320 to 394 A.D.)

"And God showed great kindness to man, in this, that He did not suffer him to continue being in sin forever; but as it were, by a kind of banishment, cast him out of paradise in order that, having punishment expiated within an appointed time, and having been disciplined, he should afterwards be recalled...just as a vessel, when one being fashioned it has some flaw, is remolded or remade that it may become new and entire; so also it happens to man by death. For he is broken up by force, that in the resurrection he may be found whole; I mean spotless, righteous and immortal."

—Theophilus of Antioch (183 A.D.)

"Wherefore also he drove him out of paradise and removed him far from the tree of life, not because He envied him the tree of life, as some dare assert, but because He pitied him and desired that he should not be immortal and the evil interminable and irremediable."

—Iraneaus of Lyons (130 to 202 A.D.)

"These, if they will, may go Christ's way, but if not let them go their way. In another place perhaps they shall be baptized with fire, that last baptism, which is not only painful, but enduring also; which eats up, as if it were hay, all defiled matter, and consumes all vanity and vice."

—Gregory of Nazianzeu, Bishop of Constantinople. (330 to 390 A.D.) Oracles 39:19

"The Word seems to me to lay down the doctrine of the perfect obliteration of wickedness, for if God shall be in all things that are, obviously wickedness shall not be in them. For it is necessary that at some time evil should be removed utterly and entirely from the realm of being."

—St. Macrina the Blessed (330 to 379 A.D.)

"For it is evident that God will in truth be all in all when there shall be no evil in existence, when every created being is at harmony with itself and every tongue shall confess that Jesus Christ is Lord; when every creature shall have been made one body."
—Gregory of Nyssa (335 to 390 A.D.)

"The wicked who have committed evil the whole period of their lives shall be punished till they learn that, by continuing in sin, they only continue in misery. And when, by this means, they shall have been brought to fear God, and to regard Him with good will, they shall obtain the enjoyment of His grace."
—Theodore of Mopsuestia (350 to 428 A.D.)

"We can set no limits to the agency of the Redeemer to redeem, to rescue, to discipline in his work, and so will he continue to operate after this life."
—Clement of Alexandria (150 to 215 A.D.)

"Do not suppose that the soul is punished for endless eons (apeirou aionas) in Tartarus. Very properly, the soul is not punished to gratify the revenge of the divinity, but for the sake of healing. But we say that the soul is punished for an aionion period (aionios) calling its life and its allotted period of punishment, its aeon."
—Olympiodorus (495 to 570 A.D.)

"Wherefore, that at the same time liberty of free-will should be left to nature and yet the evil be purged away, the wisdom of God discovered this plan; to suffer man to do what he would, that having tasted the evil which he desired, and learning by experience for what wretchedness he had bartered away the blessings he had, he might of his own will hasten back with desire to the

first blessedness…either being purged in this life through prayer and discipline, or after his departure hence through the furnace of cleansing fire."
—Gregory of Nyssa (332 to 398 A.D.)

"That in the world to come, those who have done evil all their life long, will be made worthy of the sweetness of the Divine bounty. For never would Christ have said, "You will never get out until you have paid the last penny" unless it were possible for us to get cleansed when we paid the debt."
—Peter Chrysologus, (380 to 450 A.D.)

"I know that most persons understand by the story of Nineveh and its king, the ultimate forgiveness of the devil and all rational creatures."
—Jerome (347 to 420 A.D.)

"In the end or consummation of things, all shall be restored to their original state, and be again united in one body. We cannot be ignorant that Christ's blood benefited the angels and those who are in hell; though we know not the manner in which it produced such effects. The apostate angels shall become such as they were created; and man, who has been cast out of paradise, shall be restored thither again. And this shall be accomplished in such a way, that all shall be united together by mutual charity, so that the members will delight in each other, and rejoice in each other's promotion. The apostate angels, and the prince of this world, though now ungovernable, plunging themselves into the depths of sin, shall, in the end, embrace the happy dominion of Christ and His saints."
—Jerome (347 to 420 A.D.)

"Our Lord is the One who delivers man [all men], and who heals the inventor of evil himself."
—Gregory of Nyssa (332 to 398 A.D.)

"While the devil thought to kill One [Christ], he is deprived of all those cast out of hades, and he [the devil] sitting by the gates, sees all fettered beings led forth by the courage of the Saviour."
—Athanasius (296 to 373 A.D.)

"Our Lord descends, and was shut up in the eternal bars, in order that He might set free all who had been shut up... The Lord descended to the place of punishment and torment, in which was the rich man, in order to liberate the prisoners."
—Jerome (347 to 420 A.D.)

"In the liberation of all no one remains a captive! At the time of the Lord's passion the devil alone was injured by losing all the of the captives he was keeping."
—Didymus (370 A.D.)

"While the devil imagined that he got a hold of Christ, he really lost all of those he was keeping."
—St. Chrysostom (398 A.D.)

"Stronger than all the evils in the soul is the Word, and the healing power that dwells in him, and this healing He applies, according to the will of God, to everyman. The consummation of all things is the destruction of evil...to quote Zephaniah: "My determination to gather the nations, that I am assemble the kings, to pour upon them mine indignation, even say all my fierce anger, for all the earth shall be devoured with the fire of my jealousy. For then will I turn to the people a pure language that

they may all call upon the name of the Lord, to serve Him with one consent"…Consider carefully the promise, that all shall call upon the Name of the Lord, and serve him with one consent."
—Origen (185 to 254 A.D.)

"The nations are gathered to the Judgment, that on them may be poured out the wrath of the fury of the Lord, and this in pity and with a design to heal. In order that every one may return to the confession of the Lord, that in Jesus' Name every knee may bow, and every tongue may confess that He is Lord. All God's enemies shall perish, not that they cease to exist, but cease to be enemies."
—Jerome (340 to 420 A.D., commenting on Zephaniah 3:8-10)

"Mankind, being reclaimed from their sins, are to be subjected to Christ in the fullness of the dispensation instituted for the salvation of all."
—Didymus the Blind (313 to 398 A.D.)

"So then, when the end has been restored to the beginning, and the termination of things compared with their commencement, that condition of things will be re-established in which rational nature was placed, when it had no need to eat of the tree of the knowledge of good and evil; so that when all feeling of wickedness has been removed, and the individual has been purified and cleansed, He who alone is the one good God becomes to him "all," and that not in the case of a few individuals, or of a considerable number, but He Himself is "all in all." And when death shall no longer anywhere exist, nor the sting of death, nor any evil at all, then verily God will be 'all in all'"
—Origen (185 to 254 A.D.)

"The Son "breaking in pieces" His enemies is for the sake of remolding them, as a potter his own work; as Jeremiah 18;6 says: i.e., to restore them once again to their former state."
—Eusebius, Bishop of Caesarea (265 to 340 A.D.)

"Our Savior has appointed two kinds of resurrection in the Apocalypse. 'Blessed is he that hath part in the first resurrection,' for such come to grace without the judgment. As for those who do not come to the first, but are reserved unto the second resurrection, these shall be disciplined until their appointed times, between the first and the second resurrection."
—Ambrose, Bishop of Milan (340 to397 A.D.)

"We think, indeed, that the goodness of God, through His Christ, may recall all His creatures to one end, even His enemies being conquered and subdued.... for Christ must reign until He has put all enemies under His feet."
—Origen (185 to 254 A.D.)

"For it is needful that evil should someday be wholly and absolutely removed out of the circle of being."
—Gregory of Nyssa (332 to 398 A.D.), leading theologian of the Eastern Church

"In the present life God is in all, for His nature is without limits, but he is not *all* in all. But in the coming life, when mortality is at an end and immortality granted, and sin has no longer any place, God will be all in all. For the Lord, who loves man, punishes medicinally, that He may check the course of impiety."
—Theodoret the Blessed (387 to 458 A.D.)

"When death shall no longer exist, or the sting of death, nor any evil at all, then truly God will be all in all."
—Origen (185 to 254 A.D.)

"All men are Christ's, some by knowing Him, the rest not yet. He is the Savior, not of some and the rest not. For how is He Savior and Lord, if not the Savior and Lord of all?"
—Clement of Alexandria

"God forbid that I should limit the time of acquiring faith to the present life. In the depth of the Divine mercy there may be opportunity to win it in the future."
—Martin Luther (Letter to Hanseu Von Rechenberg, 1522)

"Fire is conceived of as a beneficent and strong power, destroying what is base, preserving what is good; therefore this fire is called 'wise' by the Prophets…We say that the fire purifies not the flesh but sinful souls, not an all-devouring vulgar [earthly, natural] fire, but the 'wise fire' was we call it, the fire that 'pierceth the soul' which passes through it."
—Clement of Alexandria (Stromata VII, 2:5-12)

God's wise fire is "saving, disciplinary, leading to conversion."
—Clement of Alexandria (Stromata VI, 6)

"The Sacred Scripture does, indeed, call our God 'a consuming fire' (Heb. 12:29), and says that 'rivers of fire go before His face' (Dan. 7:10), and that 'He shall come as a refiner's fire and purify the people' (Mal. 3:2,3). As therefore, God is a consuming fire, what is it that is to be consumed by Him? We say it is wickedness, and whatever proceeds from it, such as it figuratively called 'wood, hay, and stubble' (1 Cor. 3:12-15) which denote the evil

works of man. Our God is a consuming fire in this sense; and He shall come as a refiner's fire to purify rational nature from the alloy of wickedness and other impure matter which has adulterated the intellectual gold and silver: consuming whatever evil is admixed in all the soul."
—Origen (Against Celsus, IV, 13)

"They are purged with the 'wise fire' or made to pay in prison every debt up to the last farthing...to cleanse them from the evils committed in their error...Thus they are delivered from all the filth and blood with which they have been so filthied and defiled that they could not even think about being saved from their own perdition."
—Origen (On Prayer, XXIX, 15)

"What therefore is the scope of Paul's argument in this place [1 Cor. 15:28]? That the nature of evil, at length, be wholly exterminated, and divine, immortal goodness embrace within itself every rational creature; so that of all who were made by God, not one shall be excluded from his Kingdom. All the viciousness, that like a corrupt matter is mingled in things, shall be dissolved and consumed in the furnace of purgatorial fire; and every thing that had its origin from God, shall be restored to its pristine state of purity."
—Gregory of Nyssa (Tract, in Dictum Apostoli)

APPENDIX B

76 BIBLE VERSES TO SUPPORT PATRISTIC UNIVERSALISM

Emphasis below is my own.

1. "The Father has sent the Son as Savior of the world." (1 John 4:14)

2. Jesus is "the Christ, the Savior of the world." (John 4:42)

3. "This is good and acceptable in the sight of our God our savior; Who will have all men to be saved, and to come to the knowledge of the truth. For there is one God, and one mediator between God and men, the man Christ Jesus: Who gave himself a ransom for all, to be testified in due time." (1 Tim. 2:3-6, KJV)

4. Jesus "is the propitiation for our sins, and not for ours only but also for the whole world." (1 John 2:2)

5. Jesus "did not come to judge the world but to save the *world*." (John 12:47)

6. "Jesus, was made a little lower than the angels, for the suffering of death crowned with glory and honor, that He,

by the grace of God, might taste death for *everyone*." (Heb. 2:9)

7. "Love *never* fails." (1 Cor. 13:8)

8. "With God *nothing* is impossible." (Luke 1:37)

9. "This is a faithful saying and worthy of all acceptance. For to this end we both labor and suffer reproach, because we trust in the living God, Who is the Savior of *all men*, especially of those who believe. These things command and teach." (1 Tim. 4:9-11)

10. "At the name of Jesus *every* knee should bow, of those in heaven, and those on earth, and of those under the earth, and that *every* tongue should gladly confess that Jesus Christ is Lord to the glory of God the Father." (Phil. 2:10:11)

11. "God was pleased to have all fullness dwell in Him, and through Him to reconcile to Himself *all things* on earth or in heaven, by making peace through His blood, shed on the cross. Once you were alienated from God and were enemies in your minds because of your evil behavior. But now he has reconciled you by Christ's physical body through death to present you holy in His sight, without blemish and free from accusation." (Col. 1:19, 21, 22)

12. In Jesus Christ is "the restoration of *all things*, which God has spoken by the mouth of all His holy prophets since the world began." (Acts 3:21)

13. The Gospel is "good tidings of great joy will be to *all* people." (Luke 2:10)

14. Believers in Christ are "born, not of blood, nor of the will of the flesh, nor of the will of man, but of God." (John 1:13)

15. God appointed Jesus "heir of *all things,* and through whom He made the universe." (Heb. 1:2)

16. "No one can come to Christ unless the Father who sent Him draws him." (John 6:44)

17. "And I, if I am lifted up from the earth, will draw (literally "drag" in the Greek, *helkuo*) *all mankind* unto Myself." (John 12:32)

18. "As God gave Jesus authority over *all flesh,* that he should give eternal life to as many as God have Him." (John 17:2)

19. The Father "has given *all things* into Jesus' hands." (John 13:3)

20. Jesus "was the true light which gives light to *every man* who come into the world." (John 1:9)

21. "Just as the result of one trespass was condemnation of *all men,* so also the result of one act of righteousness was justification that brings life for *all men.*" (Rom. 5:18)

22. Jesus is "able even to subdue *all things* to Himself." (Phil. 3:21)

23. Jesus came "that in the dispensation of the fullness of the times he might gather together in one *all things* in Christ, both which are in heaven and which are on earth in Him. In Him also we have obtained an inheritance, being predestined according to the purpose of Him who works *all*

things according to the counsel of His will." (Eph. 1:10, 11)

24. "The Lord is not slack concerning His promise, as some count slackness, but is longsuffering towards us, not willing that any should perish, but that *all* should come to repentance." (2 Peter 3:9)

25. "God was Christ reconciling *the world* to Himself in Christ, not counting men's sins against them. And He has committed to us the message of reconciliation. We are therefore Christ's ambassadors as though God were making His appeal through us. We implore you on Christ's behalf, be reconciled to God." (2 Cor. 5:19, 20)

26. "*All* the nations shall be blessed." (Gal 3:8)

27. "The Bread of God is He who comes down from heaven and gives Life to the *world*." (John 6:33)

28. Jesus commanded us to be like Himself and His Father: "Love your enemies, bless those who hate you, and pray for those who spitefully use you and persecute you that you may be sons of your Father in heaven." (Matt. 5:44, 45)

29. "Creation was subjected to futility, not willingly, but because of Him who subjected it in hope, because creation itself also will be delivered from the bondage of corruption into the glorious liberty of the children of God." (Rom. 8:20, 21)

30. "The Father loves the Son and has given *all things* into His hands." (John 3:35)

31. "Since by man came death, by man also came the resurrection of the dead. For as in Adam *all* died, even so in Christ *all* shall be made alive." (1 Cor. 15:22)

32. Jesus "is the image of the invisible God, the firstborn over *all creation.* For by Him all things were created that are in heaven and that are on earth, visible and invisible, whether thrones, or dominions, or principalities or powers. All things were created through Him and for Him." (Co. 1:15, 16)

33. "*All* shall know the Lord, from the least of them to the greatest of them." (Heb. 8:11)

34. "The grace of God that brings salvation has appeared to *all men.*" (Titus 2:11)

35. We are not to "repay evil for evil." (Rom. 12:17)

36. "If anyone's work which he has built endures, he will receive a reward. If anyone's work is burned, he will suffer loss; but he himself will be saved yet so as through fire." (1 Cor. 3:14, 15)

37. "Of Him and through Him and to Him are *all things,* to whom be glory forever. Amen" (Rom. 11:36)

38. "*All* Israel will be saved." (Rom. 11:26)

39. "Christ's love compels us, because we are convinced that one died for *all*, and therefore all died." (2 Cor. 5:14)

40. "How blessed is the man whose strength is in You, In whose heart are the highways *to Zion*! Passing through the valley of Baca [Gehenna] they make it a spring;

The early rain also covers it with blessings. They go from strength to strength, *Every one of them* appears before God in Zion. (Ps. 84:5-7)

41. "*All* nations shall come and worship You, for your judgments have been made manifested." (Rev. 15:4)

42. "When God's judgments are in the earth, the inhabitants of the *world* will learn righteousness." (Isaiah 26:9)

43. "Mercy shall *triumph over* (exalt over) judgment." (James 2:13)

44. "Where sin abounded, grace abounded much more." (Rom. 5:20)

45. "*Every creature* which is in heaven and on the earth and under the earth and such as are in the sea, and all that are in them, I heard saying: blessing and honor and glory and power be to Him who sits on the throne, and to the Lamb, forever and ever." (Rev. 5:13)

46. If we *really* knew the Lord, we "would not have condemned the guiltless." (Matt. 12:7)

47. "God willed to make known what are the riches of the glory of this mystery among the gentiles, which is Christ in you the hope of glory. Him we preach, warning *every man* and teaching *every man* in all wisdom that we may present every man perfect in Christ Jesus." (Col. 1: 27, 28)

48. "*All* nations whom God has made will come and worship before Him" (Ps. 86:9)

49. God's "mercy endures forever." (1 Chron. 16:34)

50. God's Spirit "will be poured out on *all flesh*." (Joel 2:28)

51. God beckons us: "Come, and let us return to the Lord, for He has torn, but He will heal us. He has stricken, but He will bind us. After two days, He will revive us. On the *third day* He will raise us up that we may live in His sight." (Hosea 6:1, 2)

52. "The Lord had made bare His Holy arm in the eyes of all the nations; and *all* the ends of the earth shall see the salvation of our God." (Isaiah 52:10)

53. "The glory of the Lord shall be revealed, and *all flesh* shall see it together; for the mouth of the Lord has spoken." (Isaiah 40:5)

54. God will "open His hand and satisfy the desire of *every* living thing." (Ps. 145:16)

55. God is "gracious in *all* His works." (Ps. 145:17)

56. "The *earth* is the Lord's and *all* its fullness, the world and those who dwell therein." (Ps. 24:1)

57. "*All* the kings of the earth shall praise you, 0 Lord, when they hear the words of your mouth." (Ps. 138:4)

58. God "reveals Himself by those who did not ask for Him: He was found by those who did not seek Him." (Isaiah 65:1)

59. "The Lord is gracious and full of compassion, slow to anger and great in mercy. The Lord is good to *all*, and His tender mercies are over *all* His works. ALL your works shall praise you, Oh Lord." (Ps.145:8-10)

60. "*All* the ends of the world shall remember and turn to the Lord, and *all* the families of the nations shall worship before You. *All* those who go down to the dust (death) shall bow before You." (Ps. 22:27, 29)

61. "Oh You Who hears prayer, to you *all* flesh will come. Iniquities prevail against me; as for our transgressions, you will provide atonement for them." (Ps. 65:2-4)

62. "Through the greatness of your power your enemies shall submit themselves to you. *all* the earth shall worship You and sing praises to you." (Ps. 66:3, 4)

63. "Through the Lord's mercies we are not consumed, because His compassions *fail not*. They are new every morning. Great is your faithfulness." (Lam. 3:21-24)

64. "The Lord will *not* cast off forever. Though He causes grief, yet He will show compassion according to the multitude of His mercies." (Lam. 3:31, 32)

65. "For I will not contend forever, Nor will I always be angry; For the spirit would fail before Me, And the souls which I have made." (Isaiah 57:16)

66. "There is no God besides Me, a just God and Savior; There is none besides Me. Look to Me and be saved, all you ends of the earth! For I am God, and there is no other. I have sworn by Myself; the word has gone out of My mouth in righteousness, and shall not return, that to me every knee shall bow, every tongue shall take an oath. He shall say, surely in the Lord I have righteousness and strength. To Him men shall come, and all shall be ashamed who are

incensed against Him. In the Lord *all* the descendants of Israel shall be justified and shall glory." (Isaiah 45:21-25)

67. "In this mountain the Lord of Hosts will make for all people a feast of choice pieces, a feast of wines on the lees, of fat things full of marrow, of well-refined wines on the lees. And he shall destroy on this mountain the surface of the covering cast over *all* nations. He will swallow up death forever, and the Lord will wipe away tears from all faces." (Isaiah 25:6-8)

68. "*All* the nations of the earth shall be blessed." (Gen. 18:18)

69. "*All* the families of the earth shall be blessed." (Gen. 12:3, 28:14)

70. "It shall come to pass the saying that is written: 'death is swallowed up in victory. Oh, Death, where is your sting Oh, Hell (Hades) where is your victory.' The sting of death is sin, and the strength of sin is the law. But thanks be to God, who gives us victory through our Lord Jesus Christ." (1 Cor. 15:54-58)

71. Of those who crucified Him (which is all of us) Jesus declared: "Father forgive them; for they know not what they do." (Luke 23:34)

72. "It is finished." (John 19:30)

73. Jesus Christ's blood was shed for the remission of sins. (Matt. 26:8)

74. "If anyone's work which he has built endures, he will receive a reward. If anyone's work is burned, he will suffer

loss; but he himself will be saved yet so as through fire." (1 Cor. 3:14, 15)

75. "Sing praise to the LORD, you His godly ones,
  And give thanks to His holy name.
For *His anger is but for a moment,*
  His favor is for a lifetime;
Weeping may last for the night,
  But a shout of joy *comes* in the morning." (Ps. 30:4-5)

76. "Give thanks to the LORD, for He is good,
  For His lovingkindness is everlasting.
Give thanks to the God of gods,
  For His lovingkindness is everlasting.
Give thanks to the Lord of lords,
  For His lovingkindness is everlasting.
To Him who alone does great wonders,
  For His lovingkindness is everlasting;
To Him who made the heavens with skill,
  For His lovingkindness is everlasting;
To Him who spread out the earth above the waters,
  For His lovingkindness is everlasting;" (Ps. 136:1-6)

ENDNOTES

CHAPTER 1

1. Hanson, J.W., *Universalism: The Prevailing Doctrine of the Christian Church During Its First Five Hundred Years*, pgs. 25-26.

2. Ibid.

CHAPTER 2

1. *The New Schaff-Herzog Christian Encyclopedia*, p. 96.

2. Ibid, p. 96.

3. Hanson, J.W., *Universalism: The Prevailing Doctrine of the Christian Church During Its First Five Hundred Years*, p. 15.

4. Ibid, p. 12.

CHAPTER 4

1. Gregg, Steve, *All You Want To Know About Hell*, p. 53.

2. For further study see: *The Doctrine of Endless Punishment* by William T.G. Shedd, p. 60; *The New Commentary on the Whole Bible*, Tyndale House, 1991; *International Standard Bible Encyclopedia*, Vol 3., 1994.

3. Jacoby, Douglas A., *What's the Truth about Heaven and Hell?*, p. 38.

4. Wright, N.T., *Christian Origins and the Question of God, Vol. 2, Jesus and the Victory of God*, p. 255.

5. Harris, R.L., Archer Jr., G.J., and Waltke, Bruce K., *Theological Wordbook of the Old Testament*.

6.   Jacoby, Douglas A., *What's the Truth about Heaven and Hell?*, p. 16.

7.   Chan, Francis and Sprinkle, Preston, *Erasing Hell*, p. 86.

8.   Gregg, Steve, *All You Want To Know About Hell*, p. 98.

9.   Ibid.

10. Zahnd, Brian, *Sinners in the Hands of a Loving God*, pp. 152-153.

11. Notation on Revelation 20:13 from *The New Testament: A Translation*, David Bentley Hart, p. 528.

12. Hanson, J.W., *Universalism: The Prevailing Doctrine of the Christian Church During Its First Five Hundred Years*, p. 62.

13. From the interview, Saturday, June 6, 2009 at: https://subversive1. blogspot.com/2009/06/interview-dr-gk-beale-part-1.html

14. From part 2 of the interview found here: https://subversive1.blogspot. com/2009/06/interview-dr-gk-beale-part-2.html

CHAPTER 5

1.   Gregg, Steve, *All You Want To Know About Hell*, p. 93.

2.   Ibid. pp. 98-99.

3.   See also 2 Chron. 16:9; Job 31:4; Jer. 16:17; Zech. 4:10.

4.   See Matt. 28:20; Heb. 13:5; Deut. 31:6, Isa. 41:10.

5.   See Acts 2:14-40; 3:12-26; 4:5-12; 7; 8:5; 10:28-47; 13:16-41; 14:3-7; 16:31; 17:22-35; 22:1-21; 23:1-6; 24:10-21; 26:2-23.

CHAPTER 6

1.   See also Matthew 3:10-12; 13:30, 42, 49-50.

2.   Gregg, Steve, *All You Want To Know About Hell*, p. 95.

CHAPTER 7

1.   Hart, David Bentley, *The New Testament: A Translation*, p. 297-298.

CHAPTER 8

1. Jersak, Brad, "Q & R: Are All People God's Children or Only Christians?" on "Christ Without The Religion" blog post, 2/26/19 at: https://tinyurl.com/y6ohm79s

2. Ibid.

3. Hart, David Bentley, *The Experience of God*, p. 8.

4. Hart, David Bentley, *That All Shall Be Saved*, pp. 40-41.

CHAPTER 9

1. Jersak, Brad, *Her Gates Will Never Be Shut*, p. 186.

CHAPTER 12

1. From a personal email correspondence with Steve Gregg, Thursday, May 22, 2019, 8:48 p.m.

CHAPTER 13

1. Kline, Steve, "New Perspective On God's Wrath", blog post, https://www.patheos.com/blogs/keithgiles/2018/09/new_perspective_gods_wrath/

2. Gregg, Steve, *All You Want To Know About Hell*, pp. 252 and 254.

3. Murray, Richard, "The Wrath of the Lamb", Facebook post, May 29, 2019.

4. Notation on Revelation 5:6 from *The New Testament: A Translation*, David Bentley Hart, p. 504.

CHAPTER 14

1. https://christianity.stackexchange.com/questions/66061/was-there-a-non-augustinian-response-to-universalism-in-the-early-church

2. https://www.ccel.org/ccel/schaff/npnf113.v.iii.xvi.html

HERETIC HAPPY HOUR

Burning questions, not people.

Heretic Happy Hour is an unapologetically irreverent, crass, and sometimes profound conversation about the Christian faith. Hosts, Matthew Distefano, Jamal Jivanjee, and Keith Giles pull no punches and leave no stones unturned. For some serious sacred cow-tipping, there's nothing better than spending an hour of your time with us.

www.heretichappyhour.com

CPSIA information can be obtained
at www.ICGtesting.com
Printed in the USA
BVHW041751201119
564386BV00014B/385/P